Exceptional Cars

Jaguar XK 120

Porter Press International

Also published by Porter Press International

The Jaguar Portfolio
Ultimate E-type – The Competition Cars
Jaguar E-type – The Definitive History (2nd edition)
Original Jaguar XK (3rd edition)
Jaguar Design – A Story of Style
Saving Jaguar

Original Scrapbooks
Stirling Moss Scrapbook 1929–1954
Stirling Moss Scrapbook 1955
Stirling Moss Scrapbook 1956–1960
Stirling Moss Scrapbook 1961
Graham Hill Scrapbook 1929–1966
Murray Walker Scrapbook
Martin Brundle Scrapbook

Great Cars Series
No. 1 – Jaguar Lightweight E-type, The autobiography of 4 WPD
No. 2 - Porsche 917, The autobiography of 917-023
No. 3 – Jaguar D-type, The autobiography of XKD 504
No. 4 – Ferrari 250 GT SWB, The autobiography of 2119 GT
No. 5 – Maserati 250F, The autobiography of 2528
No. 6 – ERA, The autobiography of R4D
No. 7 – Ferrari 250 GTO, The autobiography of 4153 GT

Exceptional Cars Series
No. 1 – Iso Bizzarrini, The remarkable history of A3C 0222

De Luxe leather-bound, signed, limited editions with leather-bound slipcase are available for most titles.
Books available from retailers or signed copies direct from the publisher.
To order simply phone +44 (0)1584 781588, fax +44 (0)1584 781630,
visit the website or email sales@porterpress.co.uk
Keep up-to-date with news about current books and new releases at:
www.porterpress.co.uk

Exceptional Cars

Jaguar XK 120
The remarkable history of JWK 651

Chas Parker & Philip Porter

Porter Press International

©Chas Parker & Philip Porter

All rights reserved. No part of this publication may be reproduced, stored in a retrieval system or transmitted, in any form or by any means, electronic, mechanical, photocopying, recording or otherwise, without prior permission in writing from the publisher

First published in March 2017

978-1-907085-56-7

Published by
Porter Press International Ltd

PO Box 2, Tenbury Wells, WR15 8XX, UK
Tel: +44 (0)1584 781588   Fax: +44 (0)1584 781630
sales@porterpress.co.uk
www.porterpress.co.uk

Edited by Ray Hutton
Design & Layout by Andrew Garman

Printed by Gomer Press Ltd

COPYRIGHT

We have made every effort to trace and acknowledge copyright holders and we apologise in advance for any unintentional omission. We would be pleased to insert the appropriate acknowledgement in any subsequent edition.

Contents

Introduction 7

The Car 8

1 XK 120 makes its entrance 10
2 The alloy competition cars 20
3 Technical analysis 24

The Races 30

Leslie Johnson 32
4 Mille Miglia, 1950 36
5 Le Mans 24 Hours 40
6 Silverstone One Hour Production Sports Car race 52
7 Tourist Trophy, Dundrod 56
8 Records at Montlhéry 62

Stirling Moss 66
9 Mille Miglia, 1951 70
10 RAC Rally of Great Britain 74

JWK 651's five brothers 80

11 A winning limited series 82

Later life of JWK 651 96

12 Over the years 98
13 Photo gallery 112

Acknowledgements 126
Index 127

Introduction

What makes a car exceptional? Its rarity? The people who drove it? The races it took part in and how many wins it achieved? Or how about the sheer diversity of the events in which it competed and its corresponding success?

JWK 651 ticks all those boxes. One of six alloy-bodied Jaguar XK120s, specially prepared for competition use by the factory in 1950, it took part in both the Mille Miglia and the Le Mans 24 Hours. Add to that the Tourist Trophy, the RAC Rally and two speed record runs at Montlhéry, one at which it averaged 107mph for 24 hours, and you have a car which boasts an unrivalled pedigree.

And then there's the driver. Leslie Johnson, the first person to win a race in an XK120. Described as charming, friendly, unassuming and courteous, he was also skilled behind the wheel and reported to be a budding Dick Seaman and as having the flair of Nuvolari. Certainly he did justice to JWK 651 during his term of ownership. He took the car to fifth in the 1950 Mille Miglia, was running third at Le Mans before retiring, finished eighth at Silverstone and finished third in the Tourist Trophy. And then, partnered by Stirling Moss no less, there was that 100mph-for-24-hours record run. There was less success when he took the car back to the Mille Miglia the following year and got caught out by oil on the road, but a return to Montlhéry resulted in achieving an average speed of 131.2mph for an hour. In 1952 the car would have finished third in the RAC Rally, but for bureaucratic nonsense.

After that, JWK 651 was acquired by Leslie Lefever, who used it as family transport and reportedly to tow his caravan, before being modified by Peter Butt, who fitted a 3.8-litre engine, wire wheels, added disc brakes all round and cut body louvres front and sides. It was later re-united with its original engine and other parts courtesy of then-owner Hugh Palmer, restored by Paul Michaels, and is now in the very capable hands of Derek Hood, of JD Classics, who has had it completely returned to its original 1950 Le Mans works specification. Not only that, he's taken it back to a couple of its old stomping grounds – Le Mans and the Mille Miglia – as well as running it at Spa, Goodwood and displaying at the Pebble Beach concours.

One thing is certain, JWK 651 *is* an exceptional car, and to see it now, just as it was in 1950, inspires a sense of awe. It's no wonder that a car with such a history deserves to have a book written about it and it has been a privilege and a delight to be able to do so.

• In its element – Leslie Johnson drives JWK 651 on the wide open spaces of Silverstone circuit, August 1950. *Guy Griffiths Collection*

Part 1
The car

It is not often that a car comes along which stops people in their tracks; which causes them to do a double-take and pause for a closer look. It is not often that a car not only enjoys huge competition success but also goes on to spawn generations of successive cars which also become game-changers in their own right. That car was the Jaguar XK 120, and it is not often that a single example of a model of car can boast as strong a heritage as the subject of this book, JWK 651. It competed in the toughest long-distance races – the Le Mans 24 Hours and the Mille Miglia. Add to that the Tourist Trophy, the RAC Rally, and speed record sessions, and you have a truly exceptional car. This is its story.

● Today JWK 651 has been lovingly and painstakingly restored to 1950 Le Mans specification by JD Classics. *John Colley*

Chapter 1
XK 120 makes its entrance

The month of October had started fine in 1948, but the night before the opening of the first post-war London Motor Show at Earls Court, the temperature fell to minus 3 degrees Centigrade. And it was not just the temperature that was causing Britain to huddle up for comfort. The country was still picking itself up from the ravages of the Second World War. Rationing remained in place and motorists had to make do with 70-octane 'pool petrol', as it was known. The main source of entertainment in the home in those days was the radio, and so a third of the population went to the cinema at least once a week.

Change was on the way as well; that year the National Health Service was established and the railways nationalised. Elsewhere in the world, Mahatma Gandhi had been assassinated following the partition of India, Israel became an independent state, and the Berlin Airlift had taken place after the Soviet Union blockaded the city.

And there was some colour in an otherwise grey world. The Games of the XIV Olympiad had been held in London during the summer, but became known as the 'Austerity Games' because of the post-war economic climate. Great Britain and Northern Ireland had won three gold, 14 silver and six bronze medals. It was a start, but Britain wanted to look more to the future, and at the London Motor Show, held at Earls Court from 27 October to 6 November, it was given a glimpse of it.

The Land Rover had already been unveiled at the Amsterdam Motor Show in April and in London 15 new models of car were introduced: Austin A70 Hampshire and A90 Atlantic, Hillman Minx, Lagonda 2.6, Morris Oxford, Morris Six, Singer SM 1500, Sunbeam-Talbot 80 and 90, Vauxhall Velox and Wyvern, Wolseley 4/50 and 6/80. Jaguar brought along two models – the Mark V and a car that stood head and shoulders above all the others on display and that would go on to lay claim to the title of greatest post-war production sports car in the world. This was the XK 120.

According to *Motor Sport*, 562,954 people attended the show. 'Without doubt, the entirely new 3½-litre XK 120 Jaguar sports two-seater stole the Show,' it reported. 'It remained a surprise until the opening day and attracted enormous attention.'

The report continued: 'The faired-in, but not sunken, headlamps offer scope for fast night driving, and the interior is simple and comfortable, while the boot offers ample luggage space. The pleasing remote gear-lever is retained and the facia carries 6,000rpm rev-counter and 120mph speedometer. Extra glass sidescreens normally occupy a zip-fastened cricket bag in the boot.' And as its caption to a photograph of the car added: 'At the basic price of £988 it represents extremely good value.' The XK 120 combined practicality and comfort with performance, all wrapped up in an exquisitely beautiful shape. It was just what was needed to put the smile back on Britain's face.

An eve-of-show announcement had already been made at the Grosvenor House hotel in London, with the press given a glimpse of the car at Henlys showroom in Park Lane, and the following statement issued:

120 M.P.H. BRITISH CAR FOR WORLD MARKETS
Record-breaking Jaguar engine to go into production
Jaguar Cars Ltd announce the introduction of a new

The prototype Jaguar XK 120 was unveiled at the 1948 London Motor Show at Earls Court and, according to contemporary reports, 'stole the show' with its stunning appearance.
Philip Porter archive

XK 120 makes its entrance

The prototype XK 120 was hastily prepared for its Earls Court debut and is seen here posed for its first official photographs. At this stage it was not a runner. *LAT*

Super Sports Car to be shown for the first time to the general public at the International Motor Exhibition at Earls Court. Powered by an entirely new engine of the type used by Lt. Col. Goldie Gardner in his recent world record achievement of 176mph, this car is capable of speeds far higher than that of any sports car yet produced for normal use.

Sensational as its performance is, the price of £988 is even more sensational, this being less than half that of cars within measureable distance of the Jaguar's specification. The car is offered with a choice of two engines, either a 4-cylinder of 2-litres capacity or a 3½-litre 6-cylinder. Eighty per cent of the first year's scheduled output has already been sold to America where the demand is insistent for a high-quality Sports Car with a racing car performance.

At the heart of the new car lay the XK engine, although the 2-litre version, as used in 'Goldie' Gardner's record-breaking run and referred to in the pre-announcement, never went into production. Designed by Bill Heynes, Claude Baily and Walter Hassan, and developed in conjunction with Harry Weslake originally with Jaguar saloon cars in mind, it was instead decided to use the 3,442cc engine for a range of limited-production sports cars, intended primarily for publicity purposes. The design for the body was drawn in a matter of weeks and the single prototype XK 120 appeared on the company's stand at the Show, having never run.

The name was derived from the estimated top speed of the car but when it did have its first outing, this turned out to be somewhat optimistic, since 102mph was the highest attainable. Among the problems discovered were that the rear wheels were fouling the bodywork, the brakes left a lot to be desired, and the handling was poor, cornering being described as unsatisfactory and the car apparently having a tendency to 'swing when decelerating from high speed'. There was obviously work still to be done.

In March 1949, development engineer Hassan produced a report entitled 'Points requiring design or improvement before release for customers or demonstration purposes'. Among the issues to be resolved was the fact that right-hand drive examples could not be built since the steering column would foul the rear carburettor. In addition, Dunlop and Lucas were developing new tyres and headlights respectively.

In April, the revised prototype XK 120 was taken to Jabbeke in Belgium for testing on a new stretch of motorway. In standard specification, with the hood down and test driver Ron 'Soapy' Sutton at the wheel, the all-important 120mph was achieved. With an undershield fitted, this went up to 123.25mph and finally, with the windscreen removed and a tonneau cover over the passenger seat, this was raised to a steady 135mph. A month later, a public demonstration before a group of invited journalists was arranged, again at Jabbeke, and the car set an official production car record of 132mph. The XK 120 was now, officially, the fastest production car in the world.

Immediately after this, Hassan, together with motoring journalist Tommy Wisdom, who was to become one of the owners of the six alloy competition cars (see Chapter 11), took a prototype XK 120, registration number HKV 500, on a long continental test run in order to assess its potential for the challenging Alpine Rally. They took the car to Switzerland and tackled a number of mountain passes. Despite having to abandon one because of a snow storm, they were convinced of the car's potential, Wisdom remarking about its stability under acceleration in low gears, enabling full throttle to be used without the tail sliding.

A chance to prove the XK 120's suitability as a competition car came at the *Daily Express* International Trophy meeting at Silverstone on 20 August 1949, at which an hour-long race for production cars was held.

At the heart of the XK 120 lay the 3,442cc straight-six XK engine, which featured an aluminium cylinder head with hemispherical combustion chambers and dual overhead camshafts. *LAT*

Service manager 'Lofty' England and Hassan tested the car beforehand at Silverstone, driving it as hard and as fast as possible to try to break it. As a result of these tests, wider brake shoes were fitted and the master cylinder moved rearwards away from the exhaust to prevent it overheating.

Three cars were entered for the One-Hour Production Car Race for leading drivers Peter Walker, Leslie Johnson and Prince Bira. They were painted, respectively, red, white and blue, and demonstrated their superiority immediately.

In its report of the meeting, *Motor Sport* said that, for many, this was the race of the day: 'At the end of the first lap, Johnson was leading by 3½ sec. from Bira, with Walker third – Jaguars 1, 2, 3! It was thought that the Jaguar drivers would scrap for 10 laps, then stay

XK 120 makes its entrance

- The XK 120's first competitive outing came at the 1949 *Daily Express* International Trophy meeting at Silverstone where Leslie Johnson, driving HKV 500 (chassis number 670002), won the One Hour Production Car Race. *Philip Porter archive*

in line-ahead formation.' The three pulled out quite a lead over the rest of the field and after only four laps were closing on the back-markers, although Walker had dropped back some way from his team-mates.

Motor Sport: 'Not only was it a fast race, but there was a full measure of excitement. On lap five Bira and Walker led, [Norman] Culpan [Frazer Nash] was third, Johnson's Jaguar was back to fourth place, these four very far ahead of the field. On the seventh lap Johnson, who had apparently contacted a straw bale with the front of his car, was in third place. Johnson and Culpan continued to battle over third place until Johnson started to pull away and closed on Walker, taking

- The owner of one of the early aluminium-bodied XK 120s, and the first customer version to reach America, was film star Clark Gable. *Press Association*

XK 120 makes its entrance

XK 120 makes its entrance

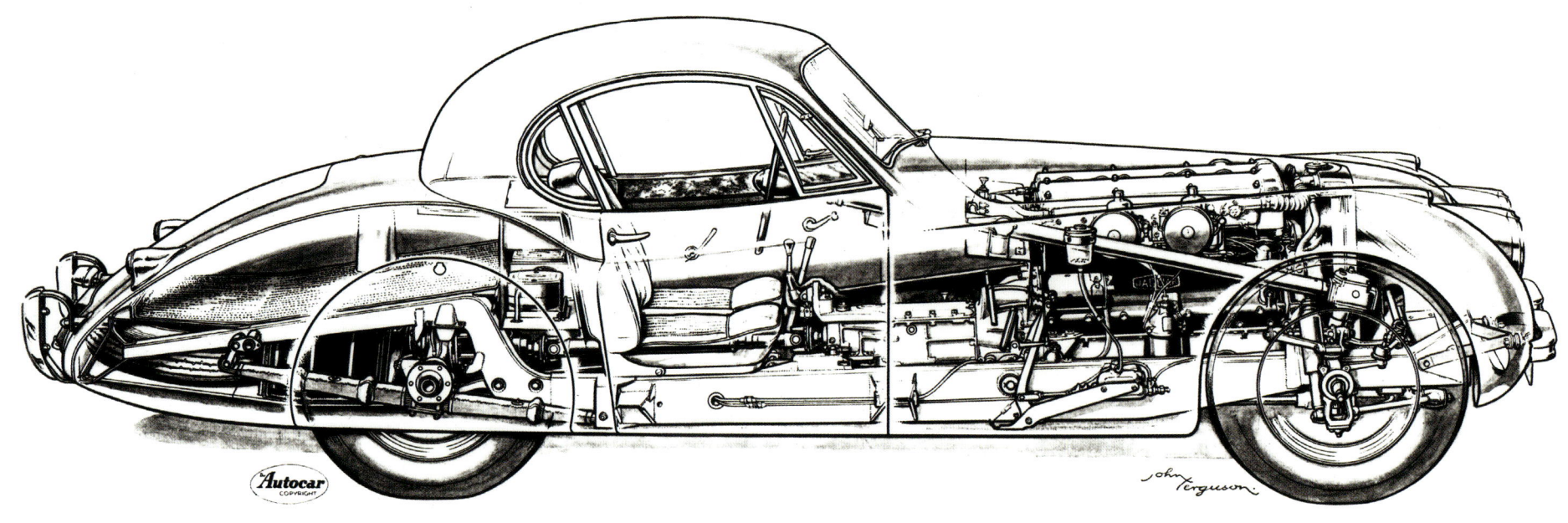

- In 1951 Jaguar added to the range of road-going XK 120s with the introduction of a closed version, the Fixed Head Coupé, which featured a plush interior, thus widening the appeal of the car. *LAT*

second place and Culpan following him through into third, then...

'Drama! Bira, Johnson pressing him really hard, was taking Woodcote Corner when the nearside rear Dunlop racing tyre burst. The blue Jaguar spun, was narrowly missed by Johnson and Walker and Bira's drive was over – but not quite. He gamely tried to jack the car up... but the jack sank into the earth and a sad man began to walk in. The mystery of why a racing tyre lasted less than 60 miles on a sports car was solved when it was found that Dunlop had fitted a touring tube! This lost Jaguar an almost-certain 1, 2, 3 victory, and the terrific publicity value of the red, white and blue cars going pass [sic] the chequered flag in line-formation.'

'Lofty' England later said that the bodywork on Bira's car had been 'a bit of a lash-up' and that the tyre had fouled on the wing support strut, causing it to wear through. Towards the end Johnson speeded up, lapping at 84.24mph, and came home ahead of Walker for a Jaguar one-two. It was an outstanding competition debut for the car.

Motor Sport featured Johnson's winning car on the cover of its September 1949 issue, with the caption: 'Setting the seal – Leslie Johnson in the 3½-litre 'XK' Jaguar winning the Production Car Race at Silverstone at 82.8mph, thus setting the seal to the prestige achieved earlier in the year at Ostend, when one of these cars did over 132mph on pump fuel. Peter Walker's Jaguar was second, 5.6 seconds behind Johnson's.'

With the XK 120 only ever intended for a limited series of around 200, and because no full production run was envisaged, the first cars were constructed in the traditional manner from aluminium panelling over an ash and steel frame. When enthusiasts started to place orders in large numbers, Jaguar had to rethink the process and pressed steel bodies were used when the car went into full production in May 1950.

This meant that only a small number of aluminium-bodied cars, around 240, were made and the majority of these were exported to the USA and Australia. With Britain needing to earn foreign currency during this post-war period, supplies of scarce raw materials were only given to companies that exported a large percentage of their goods. The XK 120 had

When the Open Two-Seater XK 120 went into full production in May 1950, pressed-steel bodies replaced the aluminium versions, of which only around 240 were built.
Philip Porter archive

A third body style for the XK 120 was introduced in 1953 in the shape of the Drop Head Coupé, which combined the appeal and performance of the Open Two-Seater with the sophistication of the Fixed Head Coupé.
Philip Porter archive

XK 120 makes its entrance

Jaguar chief engineer Bill Heynes (with cigarette) and managing director William Lyons (right) pictured in the pits at Le Mans.
Philip Porter archive

worldwide appeal and therefore served a dual prestige and financial purpose.

Meanwhile, Hassan had been head-hunted by Coventry-Climax and left Jaguar early in 1950. Before his departure, he wrote an internal memo to William Lyons, copying it to Bill Heynes and service manager 'Lofty' England. In it, he stated: 'I should have thought the firm could leave competition alone this year. Let one or two race privately – this is bound to happen anyway – and during the coming year develop a competition model.' The advice was heeded and the result was the XK 120C – the C-type.

In the meantime, Jaguar took six of the early production XK 120s – aluminium-bodied cars – and prepared them for competition use. All except one of them was sold to selected private customers, with the other being retained by the factory and prepared and modified there. These six cars, one of which was JWK 651, realised their potential and their story is told in the following chapters.

Three semi-works XK 120s took part in the 1950 Le Mans 24 Hours driven by Leslie Johnson/Bert Hadley, Nick Haines/Peter Clark and Peter Whitehead/John Marshall. After 21 hours of racing, Johnson and Hadley were in third place and catching the leading Talbot of Louis Rosier and his son Jean-Louis until clutch problems intervened and the car had to be retired. The other two finished 12th and 15th. The year culminated in victory for a young Stirling Moss in Tommy Wisdom's XK 120 in the 1950 Tourist Trophy at Dundrod in Ulster. The XK 120 went on to enjoy considerable competition success, not only on track but also in rallies such as the famous Alpine.

The success of the competition XK 120 lay in its rugged chassis, its light-alloy body and the reliability of its 3.4-litre twin-cam XK engine. The only weakness was the brakes, which suffered from a heavy wear rate and a liability to fade.

For 1951, the competition version of the car, which Hassan had advised be developed, was built with the specific intention to win at Le Mans. The XK 120C ('C' standing for competition) was based on the production car but with a lighter spaceframe chassis and more aerodynamic aluminium body. Three works cars were entered, driven by Stirling Moss/Jack Fairman, Leslie Johnson/Clemente Biondetti and Peter Walker/Peter Whitehead. The Moss car took an early lead and after four hours the three Jaguars held the top three places. However, Johnson and Biondetti retired half an hour later with low oil pressure and soon after midnight the Moss/Fairman car suffered the same fate. Walker and Whitehead pressed on though and took victory ahead of the Talbot-Lago of Pierre Meyrat and Guy Mairesse.

The road-going versions of the XK 120 were also being expanded and in 1951 Jaguar added to the range by introducing a closed version – the 'XK 120 Fixed

The winning Jaguar XK 120C, or C-type, of Peter Walker and Peter Whitehead leads the field at the start of the 1951 Le Mans 24 Hours race. *Philip Porter archive*

Head Coupé' – to join the officially termed 'XK 120 Open Two-Seater Super Sports'. Being more practical, the Coupé obviously widened the appeal of the car while still retaining all the performance advantages. The interior featured a walnut-veneered facia along with winding windows. Officially the model was only for export and just a few right-hand-drive examples were made, not all for the home market.

A Special Equipment model was launched the same year using some of the parts that had been developed for racing. Power output rose from 160bhp to 180bhp and wire wheels were introduced to help cool the drum brakes. A third body style was launched in 1953 – the 'XK120 Drop Head Coupé'. Like the roadster, it was open but it enjoyed the sophistication of the more luxurious interior of the Fixed Head combined with a lined and padded folding top and winding windows, the roadster only having a somewhat crude soft top and sidescreens.

The XK 120 certainly went a long way to help banish the post-war blues in Britain, and it also opened up the lucrative American market for Jaguar. And it's still as eye-catching today as it was in that cold October back in 1948.

Chapter 2
The alloy competition cars

When Walter Hassan departed from Jaguar, bound for Coventry-Climax, he suggested that the firm allow one or two XK 120s to be raced privately while the company spent a year developing a full competition model. This advice was heeded in part, with Jaguar taking six of the early aluminium-bodied cars and preparing them for competition use. All except one were sold to selected private customers, with the other remaining in Jaguar's ownership. All six cars were prepared by the factory for racing and rallying in 1950.

According to Andrew Whyte in his book *Jaguar Sports Racing and Works Competition Cars to 1953*, Jaguar wanted to obtain as much experience as possible in different types of events in 1950, so that problems that might not manifest themselves in ordinary testing could be identified and rectified for production models as well as the competition cars.

It was originally intended that five XK 120s be built for competition use and on 7 February 1950 a list was drawn up entitled 'Five Competition Cars: Desirable Modifications'. These included the fitting of lead indium bronze bearings; ports in the cylinder head 'modified to Silverstone standard', with the inserts radiused and the inlet manifolds matched to the heads; water pump passages streamlined; 8:1 Aerolite pistons fitted; clutch assemblies and torsional dampers tested to 8,000rpm; specially assembled floating oil filters; the fitting of anti-vibration struts to the carburettor float chambers; and an extra rear engine mounting.

All drain plugs were to be wire-locked and most nuts and bolts were either wired or split-pinned. The connecting rods were specially polished. A reverse stop mechanism, as per Silverstone cars, was fitted to avoid reverse gear being selected by mistake.

Various linings were to be tried on the brakes and new drums were made with steel back plates incorporating cooling holes. All of the suspension and steering attachment points were reamed for better fit and all bolts split-pinned. Specially-built shock absorbers were to be used, the rear axle was fitted with an 'oil baffling scheme', and a fuel pump with a dual operating system was specified. Other modifications included the fitting of a four-inch outside quick-filler 'of sufficient size and adequate venting', tanks to be made by Abbey Panels, and a special jacking system.

An extra specification sheet (see page 22) was sent by Phil Weaver to Bill Heynes on 26 April 1950, by which time a sixth chassis had been added to the original list.

Five of the cars carried consecutive chassis numbers, 660040–660044, the remaining one being 660057. They were allocated as follows:

    660040 (White) – Leslie Johnson
    660041 (Opalescent Green) – Nick Haines
    660042 (Olive Green) – Peter Walker
    660043 (Red) – Clemente Biondetti
    660044 (White) – Ian Appleyard
    660057 (Apple Green) – Tommy Wisdom

Apart from Appleyard's car, which was to be used primarily for rallying, they were prepared for racing. All the cars had factory support but only 660043, Biondetti's, remained in Jaguar's ownership. This was the first of the six to be completed, so that Biondetti could take part in the 1950 Targa Florio, having won the event for Ferrari for the previous two years.

One of the six alloy-bodied competition XK 120s, chassis number 660041, sits in the pits at Le Mans in 1950. Driven by owner Nick Haines and Peter Clark, the car ran as high as eighth at one point but was hampered by an oil leak on to the clutch towards the end and finished 12th overall.
Revs Institute for Automotive Research/Smith Hempstone Oliver

The alloy competition cars

Internal memo from Phil Weaver to Bill Heynes, dated 26 April 1950

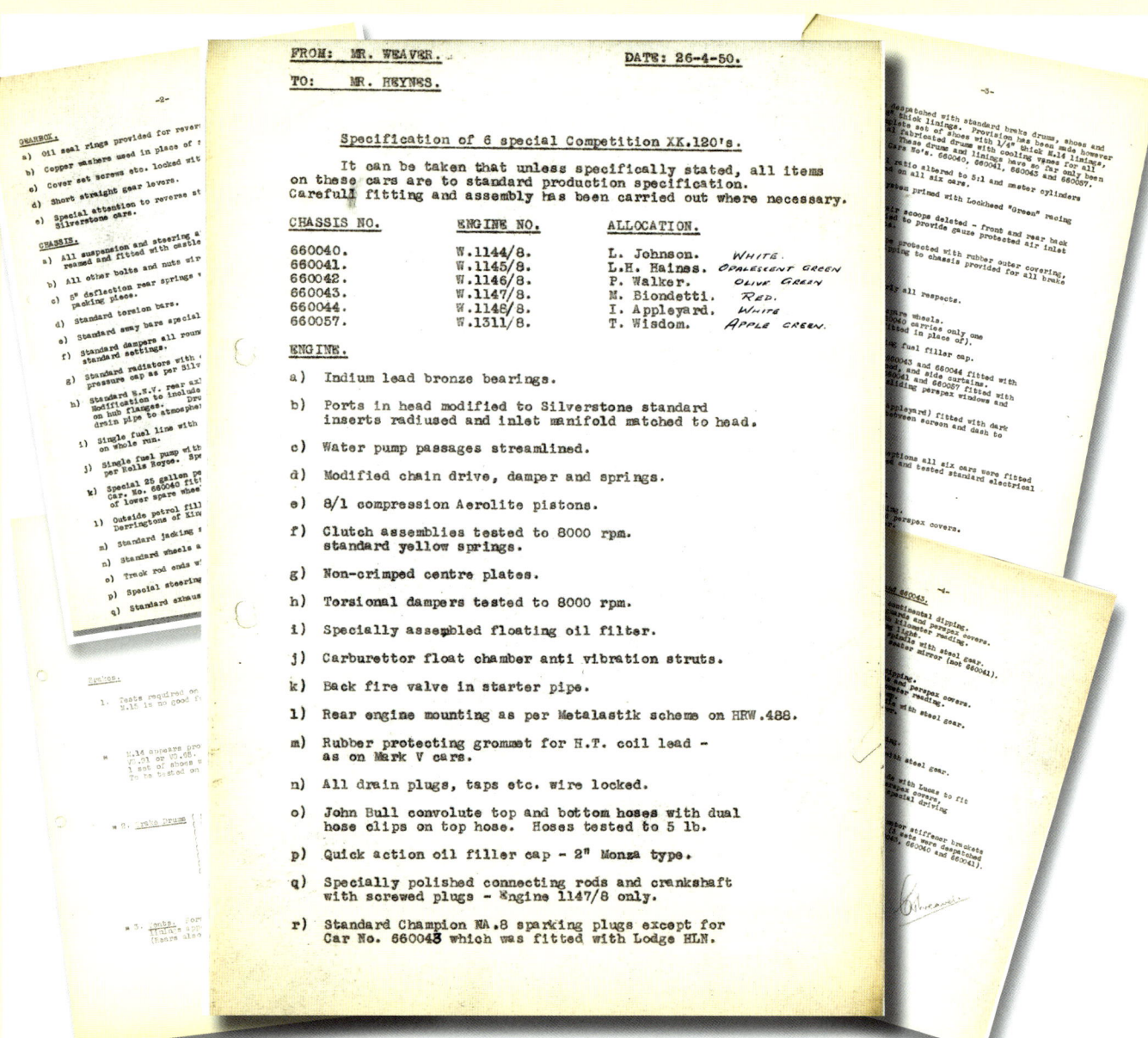

Specification of 6 special Competition XK.120's

It can be taken that unless specifically stated, all items on these cars are to standard production specification. Careful fitting and assembly has been carried out where necessary.

Engine

a) Indium lead bronze bearings
b) Ports in head modified to Silverstone standard, inserts radiused and inlet manifold matched to head.
c) Water pump passages streamlined.
d) Modified chain drive, damper and springs.
e) 8/1 compression Aerolite pistons.
f) Clutch assemblies tested to 8000 rpm. Standard yellow springs.
g) Non-crimped centre plates.
h) Torsional dampers tested to 8000 rpm.
i) Specially assembled floating oil filter.

● This internal memo from Phil Weaver to Bill Heynes, dated 26 April 1950, details the desired specification for the six alloy-bodied competition XK 120s.

Exceptional Cars

The alloy competition cars

j) Carburettor float chamber anti vibration struts.
k) Back fire valve in starter pipe.
l) Rear engine mounting as per Metalastik scheme on HRW 488.
m) Rubber protecting grommet for H.T. coil lead – as on Mark V cars.
n) All drain plugs, taps etc. wire locked.
o) John Bull convolute top and bottom hoses with dual hose clips on top hose. Hoses tested to 5 lb.
p) Quick action oil filler cap – 2" Monza type.
q) Specially polished connecting rods and crankshaft with screwed plugs – Engine 1147/8 only.
r) Standard Champion NA.8 sparking plugs except for Car No. 660043 which was fitted with Lodge HLN.

Gearbox
a) Oil seal rings provided for reverse and layshaft spindles.
b) Copper washers used in place of spring washers for set screws.
c) Cover set screws etc. locked with wire.
d) Short straight gear levers.
e) Special attention to reverse stop mechanism as per Silverstone cars.

Chassis
a) All suspension and steering attachment bolts specially reamed and fitted with castle nuts and split pins.
b) All other bolts and nuts wired or split pinned.
c) 5" deflection rear springs with standard aluminium packing piece.
d) Standard torsion bars.
e) Standard sway bars specially heat treated.
f) Standard dampers all round, but units carefully assembled, standard settings.
g) Standard radiators with completely sealed duct, and 5 lb. pressure cap as per Silverstone.
h) Standard E.N.V. rear axles all with 3.64 ratio. Modification to include oil baffles and collector rings on hub flanges. Drums modified to provide for drain pipe to atmosphere.

i) Single fuel line with outer rubber protecting tube on whole run.
j) Single fuel pump with dual operating mechanism as per Rolls Royce. Specially built and tested by S.U.'s.
k) Special 25 gallon petrol tanks with 3 point mounting. Car No. 660040 fitted with extra 10 gallon tank in place of lower spare wheel.
l) Outside petrol filler of 4" bayonet type from Derringtons of Kingston-on-Thames.
m) Standard jacking system.
n) Standard wheels and Dunlop Road Speed 6.00 x 16 tyres.
o) Track rod ends with rubber bushes.
p) Special steering units with brazed outer columns.
q) Standard exhaust system with curved tail pipe.

Brakes
a) All cars despatched with standard brake drums, shoes and M.15 3/16" thick linings. Provision has been made however for a complete set of shoes with ¼" thick M.14 linings, and specially fabricated drums with cooling vanes for all six cars. These drums and linings have so far only been fitted to Cars No's 660040, 660041, 660043 and 660057.
b) Brake pedal ratio altered to 5:1 and master cylinders repositioned on all six cars.
c) Hydraulic systems primed with Lockheed "Green" racing fluid.
d) Front brake air scoops deleted – front and rear back plates modified to provide gauze protected air inlet and exit ports.
e) Rear brake pipe protected with rubber outer covering, and better clipping to chassis provided for all brake pipes.

Body
Standard in nearly all respects. Items excepted:
a) Provision for 2 spare wheels. (Note. Car No. 660040 carries only one as 10 gal. tank fitted in place of).
b) Provision for racing fuel filler cap.
c) Car No's 660042, 660043 and 660044 fitted with standard screen, hood, and side curtains. Car No's 660040, 660041 and 660057 fitted with special hoods, and sliding Perspex windows and standard screen.
d) Car No. 660040 (Ian Appleyard) fitted with dark trimming on scuttle between screen and dash to reduce glare.

Electrical Equipment
With the following exceptions all six cars were fitted with specially assembled and tested standard electrical equipment.

Car No's 660040 and 660042
Headlamps with home dipping.
Headlamp stone guard and Perspex covers.
English M.P.H. speedometer.
Long range driving lamp.
Windscreen wiper spindle with steel gear.
Mark V mirror.

Car No's 660041 and 660043
Headlamps with continental dipping.
Headlamp stone guards and Perspex covers.
Speedometers with kilometre reading.
Long range driving light.
Windscreen wiper spindle with steel gear.
Latest extended 2 seater mirror (not 660041).

Car No 660057
Headlamps with home dipping.
English M.P.H. speedometer.
Windscreen wiper spindle with steel gear.
Standard 2 seater mirror.

(Note: Arrangements were made with Lucas to fit Headlamp stone guards and Perspex covers, long range driving lamp and special driving mirror in Italy). All cars had windscreen wiper motor stiffener brackets fitted either here or abroad. (3 sets were despatched to Italy to cover car no's. 660043, 660040 and 660041).

Chapter 3
Technical analysis

JWK 651, chassis number 660040, the subject of this book and the photographs that accompany this chapter, is one of the six competition XK 120s prepared by the Jaguar factory in 1950. As such, it is one of the first batch of XK 120s built with hand-formed aluminium alloy bodies, and includes the modifications detailed in the previous chapter.

JWK 651 nowadays is presented as raced at Le Mans in 1950. Here it is examined in technical detail, with reference to the standard production model – for the XK 120 was, in its day, the world's fastest production sports car.

Body

The first 240 XK 120s featured an ash-framed, hand-built, open two-seater body made of aluminium, mounted on a modified Jaguar Mark V chassis. In 1950, in order to meet demand, production was switched to mass-produced pressed-steel bodies, but still retaining aluminium doors, bonnet and boot lid. Although outwardly similar, the alloy and steel bodyshells are very different in construction and subtly in shape.

JWK 651's body (body number F1182) is fixed to the chassis at 14 points. The bonnet comprises a single-piece skin of aluminium with two lateral strengthening braces and an opening for the front grille. Beneath the grille, a small curved panel links the front wings. An inner wing is bolted on support brackets and extended down from the front wings, running front to rear. Steel wheelarches provide protection to the alloy wings from stone damage.

The bulkhead is fabricated in steel as a box section. In fact, the alloy cars contain a fair amount of steel, also including the inner wings and the rear bulkhead. Two adjustable diagonal tubes from the chassis frame support the bulkhead, behind which ash 'bows' attach the firewall and cockpit panel and reinforce the top of the scuttle. The door hinges are mounted on a wooden A-post faced with aluminium.

The sills are made of wood and steel and support plywood floors, one on each side. Each floor panel has a rectangular cut-out with a dished cover. With the cover removed, the jack, when inserted into the chassis jacking point, protrudes through the hole and can be wound from above.

The doors have aluminium skins and door hinges and shut pillars made of steel and wood. The rest of the door frame is ash and the inner skin aluminium. An ash frame extends rearwards from the cockpit to the tail and supports the tonneau panels surrounding the boot lid, which has a frame of ash and laminated plywood skinned in aluminium. The rear bodywork is attached at its forward section to the steel rear bulkhead.

As in all the alloy cars, the fuel tank – in this case a special item for the competition cars holding 25 gallons – is housed in the boot. While the five other competition versions made provision for two spare wheels, JWK 651 has a second 10-gallon fuel tank in the space below the floor and can carry only one spare wheel.

One point of interest is that the engine compartment of the alloy cars was painted matt black.

Not surprisingly, the steel-bodied production cars have a number of structural differences. The front

The bonnet, formed from a single sheet of aluminium, carries the grille, while the wings, including the headlamp nacelles, are connected by the lower curved body panel. The two supplementary lamps are as fitted for Le Mans, where JWK 651 ran without bumpers.
John Colley

wings are pressed in two sections and invisibly seam-welded, and the headlamp pods are made from a separate panel, spot-welded to the main wing section. A 20-inch tie-rod attaches the front wings together while an additional bracket supports the bottom of each wing just behind the wheel arch.

The bonnet is still constructed from aluminium but the underside of the outer skin is boxed at the rear, and a transverse brace follows the outline of the bonnet to about halfway back.

The firewall, bulkhead and A-post differ considerably from the alloy cars and are fabricated from small folded panels, while the sills are made entirely from steel. The doors are now all aluminium, and the floors are made from plywood.

Another difference between the two versions is that the rear wings are less bulbous on the steel-bodied cars. The rear body assembly is steel, apart from the skin of the boot lid, and the boot area is different. Instead of the petrol tank being situated in the boot, it is suspended on its own tray, ahead of the spare wheel tray; the spare wheel butts up against the curved fuel tank.

As shown here, JWK 651 has a single aero screen and fairing for the rear-view mirror for driver-only occupation during the Le Mans 24 Hours but contemporary photographs show that it was driven to the race with the standard split windscreen in place.

The early cars were provided with a lightweight canvas top and detachable sidescreens that stowed behind the seats. Since there are no external door handles, entry with the hood in place required the interior pull cord to be reached through a flap in the sidescreens. JWK 651 was one of the three competition cars to be supplied fitted with 'a special hood and sidescreens with sliding Perspex windows'. The original roof and sidescreens no longer exist.

All these cars had removable rear wheel spats. JWK 651 ran at Le Mans without them – to make wheel changes easier – and they were omitted from the XK 120 specification when, from 1951, optional centre-lock wire wheels were fitted; there would have been insufficient clearance for the chromed, two-eared Rudge-Whitworth knock-off hubs with the spats in place.

Chassis

The chassis consists of two main steel box sections running from the front of the car to about two-thirds of the way back, splaying outwards as they run rearwards. These main members are joined by a cross-member a short distance from the front and behind this are mounting points for the top wishbone, radiator, engine and dampers. The body mounting brackets are further back.

A larger box-section cross-member is located around the centre, between the two main members. This includes a large hole for the exhaust to pass through and carries attachment points for the torsion bars, gearbox and prop-shaft tunnel. Two smaller box-section members are sleeved into the main members at the rear and these sweep up steeply, bent ever more sharply horizontal and then fall away to the rear, tapering gently. This S-shaped profile behind the seat area is in order to clear the axle. A section of folded steel acts as a cross-member between the two at the point of maximum curvature.

Today it can be seen that, at some point in its history, JWK 651 had mounting points for an undertray fitted. It is quite likely that this was an attempt at streamlining the underside of the car for the 1950 record attempt at Montlhéry (see Chapter 8). The chassis also has mounting points for an extra pair of shock absorbers, which would have been fitted either for the Mille Miglia or the Montlhéry record runs.

All XKs carry a chassis, or identification, plate, usually attached to the bulkhead in the engine compartment. This bears the chassis, engine, body and gearbox numbers as well as information on inlet and exhaust valve clearances and lubricant recommendations.

Interior

In a standard XK 120, bench-like seats extend across the width of the cockpit, split in the middle by the prop-shaft tunnel. Cushion and fold-forward backrests are upholstered in leather, which also covers the dashboard, door casings and cockpit rolls; other areas, such as the scuttle and footwells, are trimmed in artificial materials. JWK 651 had individual bucket seats from the start of its racing career, faithfully reproduced in durable cloth for the restoration to Le Mans specification.

The carpets are Rexine-bound, with thick insulating felt under the toeboard and gearbox tunnel area. The gear lever and handbrake have leather gauntlets to cut out road noise and draughts. The doors have a rectangular pocket, covered by a flap.

A central instrument panel contains all the gauges, warning lights and switches. On the right is a Smiths speedometer, reading to 140mph, while on the left sits a 6,000rpm rev counter. Arranged in a triangle between these two are, at the top, a combined oil pressure and temperature gauge, a combined petrol and oil level gauge (left) and an ammeter.

Engine

The 3.4-litre straight-six XK engine featured a cylinder block made from chrome cast iron, an aluminium die-cast sump, and a detachable cylinder head made of high-tensile-strength aluminium alloy, with hemispherical combustion chambers and dual overhead camshafts. Aluminium was chosen mainly for its lightness but also for its high rate of heat conductivity.

The induction system and combustion chamber were designed in collaboration with H. Weslake and Company and the overhead valves sit at an angle of 70degrees with the spark plug offset between them. The valves are operated by the cams driving directly on

The interior of the alloy competition cars was mostly standard XK 120 but JWK 651 had individual bucket seats, specified by its first owner Leslie Johnson. In Le Mans trim, a single aero screen and fairing for the rear-view mirror replace the full-width windscreen.
John Colley

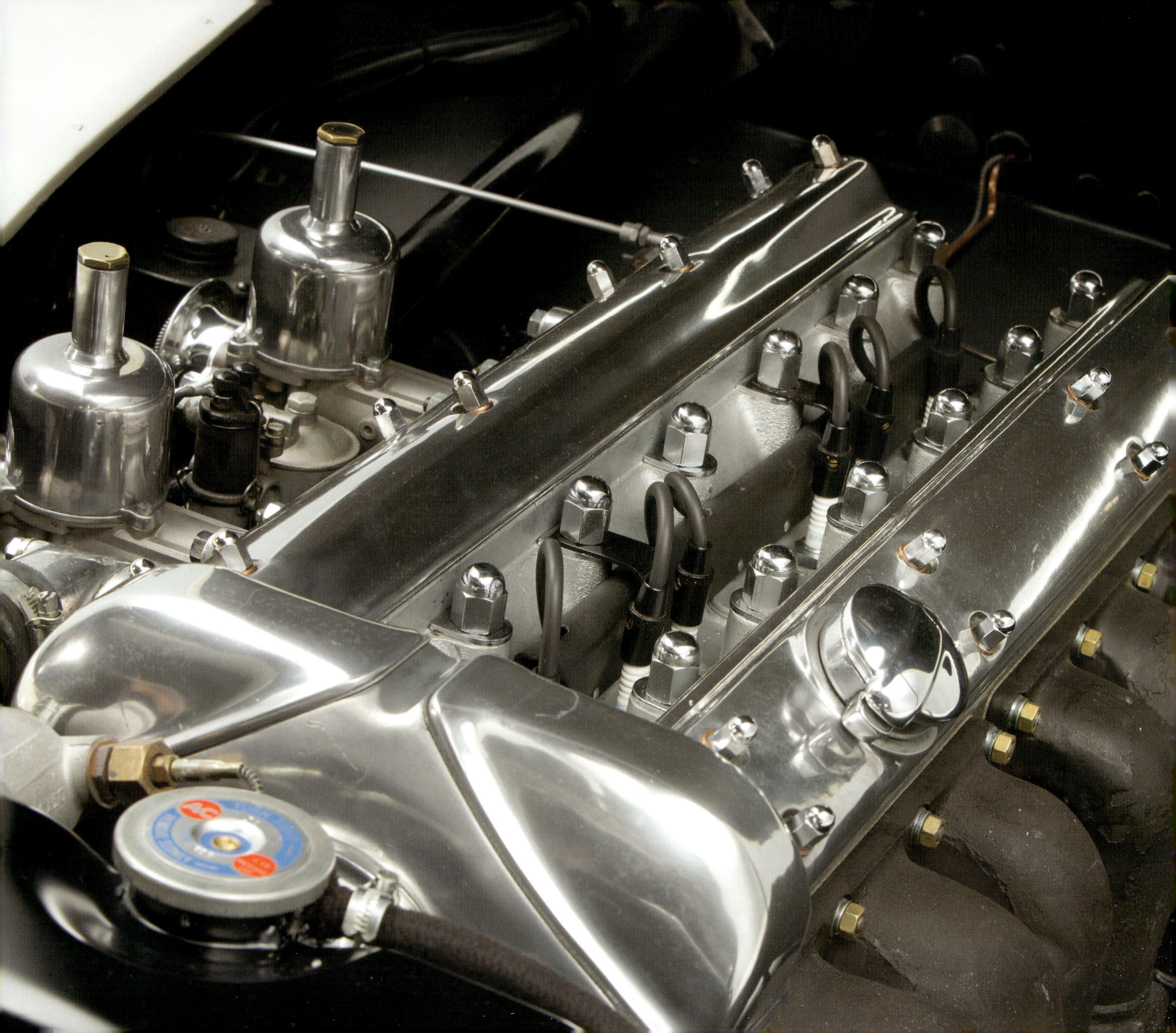

Technical analysis

Specification

Engine
Six cylinders; Bore and stroke: 83mm x 106mm; Swept volume: 3,442cc; Maximum bhp: 160bhp at 5,200rpm Maximum bmep and torque: 140 lb per sq in. and 195 lb/ft at 2,500rpm; Compression ratio: 8:1; Seven-bearing crankshaft Twin overhead camshafts driven by two-stage duplex roller chain; Twin 1 3/4 In.SU H6 carburettors

Clutch
Borg and Beck single dry-plate 10in. diameter

Gearbox
Four speeds and reverse with constant load synchromesh on top, third and second; Ratios: top – 1:1; third – 1.367:1; second – 1.982:1; first and reverse – 3.375:1

Rear axle
ENV banjo type with hypoid gears. Ratio 3.64:1

Suspension
Front – wishbones and torsion bars with anti-roll bar
Rear – semi-elliptical springs in conjunction with Hotchkiss drive

Steering
Burman recirculating ball

Brakes
Lockheed hydraulic, two leading shoe at front, leading and trailing shoes at rear. Brake drum diameter and effective width: 12in. x 2¼in. Friction area: 207 sq in.

Fuel supply
From 25 gallon rear tank with 10 gallon reserve supply; SU electric pump

Tyres
Dunlop Road Speed 6.00in x 16in. Pressed steel, bolt-on disc wheels with 5in. wide rims, five-stud mounting

Dimensions
Wheelbase: 102in.; Front track: 51in.; Rear track: 50in. Overall width: 61in.; Overall length: 168in.; Overall height: 50in.; Turning circle: 31ft; Ground clearance: 7½in., Weight, dry: 2,800lb

● Neat and tidy underbonnet, with the magnificent XK engine fed by twin SU H6 carburettors and two exhaust manifolds serving three cylinders each. Spark plugs are easy to access on this upright straight-six engine.
John Colley

to chill cast-iron cylindrical tappets and the camshafts are driven by two-stage duplex roller-chains. The 1¾-inch inlet valves are made from silicon chrome steel while the slightly larger $1\frac{7}{16}$-inch exhaust valves are austenitic steel and the valve seats, special high-expansion cast-iron alloy.

The seven-bearing crankshaft, made of manganese molybdenum steel, is of conventional design, although it features large, 2¾-inch main bearings and the oil pump is driven off the front of the crankshaft.

JWK 651 was supplied with engine number W1144-8. Officially, it delivered 160bhp at 5,200rpm but according to Andrew Whyte's book *Jaguar Sports Racing and Works Competition Cars to 1953,* when, after Le Mans, the engine was rebuilt and bench-tested, it was giving 165.5bhp at 5,200rpm.

In original specification, the engine had the standard compression ratio of 8:1. Most of the early cars were exported but a low-compression version of 7:1 was kept for the UK market where post-war austerity measures meant only poor-quality 70-octane 'pool petrol' was available.

When the XK 120 was introduced it had twin side-draft 1¾-inch SU H6 carburettors, recognisable by the tall 'chimney pot' tops, along with a third auxiliary starting carburettor. At first steel cars incorporated the same carburettors but these were replaced from April 1950 by shorter dash pots.

Transmission

The XK 120 is fitted with what was known as a 'Moss box' – a four-speed single-helical (SH) synchromesh gearbox designed and built by Moss Gears. A Hardy Spicer prop-shaft connected to the rear axle which was manufactured by ENV and available in five different ratios: 3.27:1, 3.64:1, 3.92:1, 4.30:1 and 4.56:1. The standard specification, continued for the competition cars, including JWK 651, was 3.64:1.

Suspension

The independent front suspension of the XK 120 uses torsion bar springs in conjunction with top and bottom wishbones and anti-roll bar. Rear suspension is by a solid rear axle with seven-leaf semi-elliptical springs.

Steering

The XK 120 has a Burman recirculating ball system, the steering unit for which is carried in a trunnion on the driver's side top wishbone bracket. A drop arm was connected by a tubular rod to a corresponding slave drop arm on the opposite side of the chassis. These linkages connected to the steering arms attached to the uprights, via two ball joints. The steering column is telescopically adjustable and the Bluemel 17-inch steering wheel has an integral boss.

Brakes

All XK 120s were fitted with Lockheed hydraulic 12-inch drum brakes, front and rear. The rears used leading and trailing shoes in each drum, while the fronts had a pair of identical shoes. JWK 651 was among the first three cars to be fitted with thicker, ¼-inch linings and specially fabricated drums with cooling vanes. The brakes were still prone to fade and so some cars were fitted with Alfin (Aluminium FINned) brake drums to combat this.

Wheels and tyres

JWK 651, like all early XKs, was originally fitted with 6.00 x 16 cross-ply tyres on pressed steel disc wheels of 16-inch diameter and 5-inch width, with five-stud fixings.

For standard cars, the wheels were finished in the body colour of the car and fitted with 'wheel discs', or hub caps as they are now known, mainly chromed but with the sunken area in body colour and a badge with the word 'Jaguar' on a black background at the centre.

The standard wheel width was increased by ½-inch, to 5½ inches, in December 1952/January 1953. Chromium-plated 54-spoke wire wheels became optional from 1951 onwards.

After its three-year racing and rally career, JWK 651 was fitted with wire wheels (see Part 4) but has now been returned to steel disc wheels without hub caps, as raced at Le Mans in 1950.

Part 2
Races, rallies and records

In Leslie Johnson's hands JWK 651 enjoyed a varied and successful competition career over a three-year period. The 1950 season was the busiest time, with Johnson driving the car at Le Mans (retired with a broken clutch), the Mille Miglia (fifth overall), in the production sports car race at Silverstone (eighth), the Tourist Trophy at Dundrod (seventh) and at the banked Montlhéry track in France where, partnered with Stirling Moss, he averaged over 100mph for 24 hours. The following year saw a return to both the Mille Miglia (crashed) and Montlhéry (over 130mph solo for one hour) while the car's final competitive outing in period was the 1952 RAC Rally, where a technical infringement cost Johnson a probable third place. The man and the car were nothing if not versatile.

● Leslie Johnson, partnered in JWK 651 by Bert Hadley, ran as high as second in the 1950 Le Mans 24 Hours before dropping back and having to retire with a broken clutch with only three hours to go.
Klemantaski Collection/ Louis Klemantaski

Leslie Johnson

Leslie Johnson, the first owner of JWK 651, was described by motor racing photographer Guy Griffiths as a 'charming, friendly, unassuming and courteous man'. He was not only the first person to win a race in an XK 120, but also the first to race an XK 120 abroad.

Johnson was born on 22 March 1912 in Walthamstow, London. His father, a cabinet-maker, died while Johnson was still in his teens and so he took charge of the family firm, running it with care and concern for his employees and turning it into a successful furniture business.

He competed regularly in pre-war rallies driving a BMW 328, winning both the Scottish Rally and Torquay Rally in 1937, and finishing third in the RAC Rally in 1938 and 1939.

After the war he campaigned a Talbot-Lago T150C as well as the BMW, finishing first and second respectively in them at the Shelsley Walsh hill climb on 1 June 1946, followed by second at Prescott on 28 July in the Talbot. On 7 September he set FTD at Bo'ness in the Talbot on his first visit to the course.

Johnson also raced the Talbot, both as a sports car

- Described as charming, friendly, unassuming and courteous, Leslie Johnson was not only the first person to win a race in an XK 120, albeit not JWK 651, but also the first to race one abroad. *LAT*

Winning the 1948 Spa 24 Hours with St John 'Jock' Horsfall in a specially-bodied Aston Martin DB1 was a major success for Johnson, who was invited to join the Jaguar works team the following year. *LAT*

Leslie Johnson

Johnson's best result at Le Mans came in 1952 when he shared a Nash-Healey with Tommy Wisdom and finished third overall. *The Revs Institute for Automotive Research/George Phillips*

Spa 24 Hours in an Aston Martin DB1, partnered by St John Horsfall.

In 1949 Johnson persevered with the ERA, finishing third in both the Goodwood Chichester Trophy and the British Empire Trophy at Douglas, Isle of Man. He drove a works Aston Martin DB2 at Le Mans, paired with Charles Brackenbury, but they retired after only six laps. Later he married Brigit, the widow of one of his team-mates, Pierre Maréchal, who perished in that race.

That year Johnson also joined the works Jaguar team. He won on his first outing in an XK 120 (HKV 500) at Silverstone in the production sports car race at the *Daily Express* Trophy meeting, despite an early collision with a Jowett Javelin that dropped him to fifth place. He took an XK 120 to the USA at the end of the year and finished fourth (and first in the production sports car class) at Palm Beach in January 1950. It was an important event that helped launch the XK 120 on to the lucrative American market.

Johnson had already established close links with Jaguar, having become firm friends with Bill Heynes, the Chief Engineer, and he had lent his BMW 328 to the company to study during the planning stage of the XK 120. It is not surprising, therefore, that on his return to the UK in early 1950 he became one of the chosen recipients of the competition-prepared alloy XK 120s. His competition exploits with JWK 651, of course, are detailed in this book.

Johnson was also kept busy in other machinery. He was entered at Le Mans in 1951 in a Jaguar C-type but the car retired with Clemente Biondetti at the wheel before he had a chance to drive it. At the Tourist Trophy at Dundrod he was off-form and handed the car over to Tony Rolt. He had also been due to drive the V16 BRM at the 1951 Italian Grand Prix but the car blew up in pre-race practice with Hans Stuck at the wheel, Johnson

and a single-seater, simply removing the mudguards as required. He competed in three Grands Prix in it in 1947 with his best result being sixth at the Jersey International Road Race.

Prior to that, in 1946, he finished second at the Brussels International Sports Car race at Spa in the BMW and was described by the *The Motor* as a 'budding Dick Seaman', its report of the event stating: 'Sommer and Chiron danced with fiendish glee as Johnson shot by and took the esses in a single controlled slide.

Chiron said he had the flair of Nuvolari. Sommer, inarticulate with emotion, kissed the poor chap.'

Between 1946 and 1950, Johnson raced a Delage, the Talbot-Lago and an ERA in single-seater events, the latter having come about when he took over the struggling ERA concern in 1948. He entered the British Grand Prix at Silverstone that year and started fifth on the grid, but retired when a drive-shaft broke.

He had more success elsewhere that year, coming third in the Manx Cup in an Alvis and winning the

In his last Mille Miglia, in 1953, Johnson drove his new C-type Jaguar but failed to finish.
The Revs Institute for Automotive Research/Rudolfo Mailander

having been delayed on his way to the circuit.

Although no longer a works driver, he continued to compete throughout 1952 in rallies and races and took part in the Montlhéry record run for Jaguar along with a team of drivers comprising Stirling Moss, Bert Hadley and Jack Fairman, to average 100mph for a week in an XK 120 FHC. He drove a works Nash-Healey in the Mille Miglia and then at Le Mans in the same car he finished third overall and first in class.

Johnson was plagued by ill-health throughout his life and in 1953, on advice from his doctor, he sold his business interests. He bought a C-type but hardly ran it and then, while competing in the 1954 Monte Carlo Rally, driving a Sunbeam Talbot, he collapsed with a heart attack. Despite this, he urged his fellow team members, including Stirling Moss and Sheila van Damm, to get to the finish, thus winning the team prize.

Needless to say he retired from competition permanently and bought a farm in Gloucestershire. Johnson died on 8 June 1959, aged just 47.

Chapter 4
Mille Miglia
23 April 1950

The Mille Miglia, or 'Thousand Miles', was essentially a one-lap race around Italy on open roads through towns and villages and over unmade mountain passes. The route ran from Brescia in the north, down the Adriatic coast, over the Apennines to Rome, where the cars turned back north and made their way, via a number of different routes over the years, back to Brescia. It was open to production models only and the numbers on the cars reflected their starting time, so a car that set off at ten past six in the morning was numbered 610. This gave spectators the chance to assess who was making the most progress as the cars passed. The event was held on 24 occasions between 1927 and 1957.

The number 17 is regarded as unlucky in Italian culture. In order to avoid reference to it, and hence attempt to side-step bad fortune, the 17th running of the gruelling event was named *La Mille Miglia del 1950 per la Coppa Franco Mazzotti,* after one of the founders of the event. Sadly, the ruse didn't work. The race, held on 23 April 1950, and run over normal roads through cities, towns and villages, was beset with appalling weather that resulted in a large number of crashes, some of them fatal.

It was at this event that JWK 651 made its competition debut in the hands of Leslie Johnson and his riding mechanic John Lea. The car had a full windscreen fitted for the race, but poor Johnson had to drive for two-thirds of the event propped up in order to see over the screen whenever it rained, the wipers having stopped working. Despite this, JWK 651 was still the leading Jaguar to finish. His fifth place, beaten only by three Ferraris and a works Alfa Romeo, was to be the highest an XK would ever achieve at this car-breaking event. It would also prove to be the highest (equal) finish ever by a British car and driver combination.

A new route had been chosen for the 1950 event, starting as usual at Brescia and heading east to Padua, via Verona, then south down the Adriatic coast through Ravenna, before turning inland at Pescara to Rome, then north to Pisa, over the Futa and Raticosa passes to Bologna, then to Modena and Parma and returning to Brescia.

A record field of 383 (or 375, depending on which report you read) started the event, due partly to an 'open-door' policy of admitting anyone, instigated the previous year. Ferrari had no fewer than 16 V12-engined cars entered, 11 of which were 2-litre 166 S models, in both open and closed forms. There were also three 195 S cars with 2.3-litre engines and two 3.3-litre 275 S models for Alberto Ascari and Luigi Villoresi. Four of the Ferrari drivers were the Marzotto brothers, Giannino, Vittorio, Umberto and Paolo, whose family owned a textile empire and a chain of hotels and who drove Scuderia Marzotto/Ferrari-entered cars.

Alfa Romeo provided the main opposition, with Franco Rol and Juan Manuel Fangio in 2.5-litre 6C 2500s in short-chassis coupé form, a 6C 3000 with a 3-litre experimental engine for Consalvo Sanesi, and a rebodied *Tipo* 412 4.5-litre V12 for Felice Bonetto.

Five of the new Jaguar XK 120s were entered for four-times winner Clemente Biondetti (660043), Leslie Johnson (660040), Tommy Wisdom (660057), Nick Haines (660041) and the Swiss driver 'Ideb' with

Seen lining up for its first competitive outing, the 1950 Mille Miglia, JWK 651 was fitted with a full windscreen and fabric roof. The car, with Leslie Johnson at the wheel accompanied by John Lea, carries the number 735, corresponding to a starting time of 7.35 in the morning. *Archivio Novafoto-Sorlini/ Giorgio Nada Editore*

Mille Miglia

a privately prepared standard car. According to *The Autocar*, Biondetti's Jaguar was fitted with a radio 'in order to receive race bulletins *en route*'.

There were four Healeys, including Donald Healey and his son Geoffrey in a Nash-Healey (a Healey Silverstone with 3.8-litre Nash engine). The bulk of the field was made up of Fiats and Lancias competing in the national touring category and these cars set off first from Brescia, at midnight, when the weather was still clear, each with its start time painted on its side. By the time the bigger-engined sports cars arrived at the start line a few hours later, however, they were greeted by fog and torrential rain.

Film of the race shows spectators lining the streaming wet roads, huddled underneath umbrellas, and Biondetti waving to the huge crowd braving the weather around the start-line as he set off in his XK 120.

The roads were treacherous and one of the first to fall victim was the Ferrari 166 of Aldo Bassi, who crashed fatally. Another incident befell Prince Lanza, one of the organisers of the Targa Florio, whose Cisitalia coupé rolled down an embankment but without causing serious injury to the driver. Soon afterwards, however, Phillip Wood crashed his Healey at the same point, his co-driver Peter Monkhouse sustaining fatal head injuries while Wood himself suffered a broken leg. The 17th running of the Mille Miglia was indeed proving unlucky for some.

But the greasy conditions suited the nimble blue 2.3-litre Ferrari 195 S *berlinetta* of Giannino Marzotto,

• Competitors encountered atrocious weather in the 1950 Mille Miglia but Leslie Johnson and and John Lea came to the start with JWK 651's roof removed for optimum visibility. *Archivio Novafoto-Sorlini/ Giorgio Nada Editore*

who was driving wearing a double-breasted suit, with silk tie and waistcoat. He led the more powerful 275 S Ferraris of Villoresi and Ascari at Ravenna, 118 miles from the start, by two and a half minutes, with Dorino Serafini's Ferrari 195 S fourth and Fangio's Alfa 6C 2500 fifth. Biondetti, in the first of the Jaguars, was seventh.

Villoresi made the most of the larger engine in his Ferrari to take the lead from Marzotto down the Adriatic coast and still led at Pescara, despite stopping to change a tyre, having averaged 92mph over the first 375 miles. Serafini's Ferrari was now third, followed by Ascari who was suffering tyre problems, losing treads.

On the leg from Pescara, over the Apennines to Rome and the west coast, both Villoresi and Ascari retired their 275 S barchettas with broken transmissions, the new engines proving too powerful for the chassis. This allowed Marzotto back into the lead by the time he reached Rome, a minute ahead of Serafini with Fangio now up to third in his Alfa, followed by Cortese's Frazer Nash and then five Jaguars with Johnson at the front. Earlier, Fangio had been passed for third place by his team-mate, Bonetto, who retired shortly afterwards.

The accidents continued. Sanesi crashed his 3-litre Alfa between Rovigo and Ferrara, injuring himself and co-driver Bianchi, and Rol retired his Alfa when the brakes failed. Robin Richards also crashed in his Healey, sustaining a broken leg, while the Ferrari of Umberto Marzotto ended up against a tree, and Paulo Marzotto also ran off the road, both without injury.

For their brother Giannino, though, it was a different story. He crossed the line in Brescia at around 9pm, followed by Serafini second and Fangio third, while the class-winning Ferrari 166 S of Giovanni Bracco was fifth.

Johnson and Lea brought the wiper-less JWK 651 home in fifth place, Johnson having driven the entire distance. Of the other Jaguars, Biondetti was delayed by a broken rear spring but still managed to limp home in eighth place and 'Ideb' finished 16th. Wisdom eventually retired his XK 120 only 30 miles from the finish with transmission problems, having already been delayed by a loose wheel and a sticking throttle, while Haines crashed into a wall.

At the end, Marzotto could be seen smiling in his dark suit, any superstitions he might have had about the number 17 having been vanquished.

Results

1	724	Giannino Marzotto/Marco Crosara (Ferrari 195 S Berlinetta Touring)	13h 39m 20s (76.79mph)
2	733	Dorino Serafini/Etorre Salani (Ferrari 195 S Berlinetta Touring)	13h 46m 53s
3	730	Juan Manuel Fangio/Augusto Zanardi (Alfa Romeo 6C 2500 Competizione Berlinetta)	14h 02m 05s
4	711	Giovanni Bracco/Umberto Maglioli (Ferrari 166 MM Barchetta Touring)	14h 07m 23.6s
5	**735**	**Leslie Johnson/John Lea (Jaguar XK 120)**	14h 29m 27s
6	658	Franco Cortese/Zaccaria Teravazzi (Frazer Nash Le Mans Replica)	14h 33m 59s
7	540	Luigi Fagioli/Francesco Diotallevi (OSCA MT4 1100)	14h 34m 44.4s
8	729	Clemente Biondetti/Gino Bronzoni (Jaguar XK 120)	14h 38m 39.8s
9	722	Vittorio Marzotto/Paulo Fontana (Ferrari 195 S Barchetta Fontana)	14h 39m 02.6s
10	456	Adolfo Schwelm-Cruz/R. De Simone (Alfa Romeo 6C 2500 SS Coupé Touring)	14h 45m 51.2s

John 'Jack' Lea

John Lea joined the racing and experimental department at Lea-Francis (no relation) in 1928, attending many races and acting as riding mechanic for a number of drivers. When Lea-Francis went into receivership in 1931 he moved to C.T. Delaney and Sons before joining ERA at its inception. There he was involved with the preparation and development of all cars up to the E-type model.

During the Second World War Lea worked as a service engineer for the Bristol Aeroplane Company before joining Jaguar as a mechanic in the experimental department, working on the XK 120 and later the C-type. He joined Leslie Johnson on a trip to Florida for a race on the streets of Palm Beach in January 1950 and while there Johnson asked Lea if he would accompany him on the Mille Miglia that year. Prior to this, Lea drove Clemente Biondetti's XK 120 (660043) to Italy for the Targa Florio (see Chapter 11).

As riding mechanic to Johnson on the Mille Miglia, Lea was able to savour a fine fifth place in JWK 651. In Jaguar Sports Racing and Works Competition Cars to 1953, Andrew Whyte stated that 'Lea's sorties to the continent had been the first of its kind by a Jaguar racing mechanic'.

Further such excursions were to follow but in 1952 Lea, deciding he had had enough of big organisations, left Jaguar to set up his own business. He bought a garage in the Cotswolds at Gretton in Gloucestershire, close to Prescott hill climb, where he prepared competition cars for a number of privateer drivers, including long-time Jaguar employee Bob Berry.

Lea died, aged 88, in 1998.

Chapter 5
Le Mans 24 Hours
25–26 June 1950

Les Vingt-Quatre Heures du Mans was conceived as a demonstration of reliability for production cars, rather than an actual race. As such, at the first event in 1923, each car was set a minimum distance that it was required to complete during the 24 hours, according to its engine capacity. The 'winner' would be the car that exceeded its target distance by the greatest amount rather than the one that completed the greatest actual distance during that time. Those cars that managed to achieve or exceed their target distance were to be eligible for the following year's event, the overall winner, and recipient of the Rudge-Whitworth Cup, being declared after three years.

The event quickly captured the imagination of the press and public alike, with thousands attending. During these early years the nature of both the track and the race evolved, with an overall winner for each year's race being declared from 1928 onwards. In the period up to the Second World War the names of Bentley and Alfa Romeo became synonymous with Le Mans and to win the 24 Hours became the ultimate accolade for a car manufacturer.

During the war the adjacent airstrip suffered bomb damage and the area was mined, so it was not until 1949 that the first post-war 24 Hours was held. It was won by Luigi Chinetti and Lord Selsdon in a Ferrari 166 MM – the first of many Ferrari victories through the 1950s and 1960s.

The appearance of Jaguar at Le Mans in 1950, with its three factory-prepared XK 120s for selected private entrants, was big news. The company had began series production of the XK 120 only a month earlier. Since Jaguar did not have a competition department of its own at this time, the cars were registered as private entries, even though they were prepared by the factory and operated at the circuit by Jaguar's 'Lofty' England (Service Manager) and Bill Heynes (Chief Engineer).

The three cars were those owned by Leslie Johnson (660040), Nick Haines (660041) and Peter Walker (660042). As Walker was otherwise committed that weekend, his car was entrusted to Peter Whitehead. Johnson persuaded famous pre-war works Austin driver Bert Hadley out of retirement to join him, while Haines was paired with Peter Clark and Whitehead with John Marshall.

Heynes later commented that the three cars 'were probably the most standard that had ever been run in that race'. Even so, they were fitted with optional extras such as an aero screen, mirror cowl, lightweight bucket seats and 25-gallon fuel tank with quick-action filler. Complete with a box of tools mounted next to the driver, since only those carried in the car could be used during the race, even at pit stops, the cars weighed a hefty 30cwt (1,524kg).

On 7 June, Haines wrote to 'Lofty' England with a list of suggested spares and the comment: 'Please make every effort to ensure a really good set of lights for the car, those at present on it are hopelessly inadequate'.

Haines and Clark were allocated race number 15, Whitehead and Marshall 16, and Johnson and Hadley, in JWK 651, 17.

Opposition came from the previous year's winner, Ferrari, which had two new 195 S models, with 2.4-litre

For Le Mans 1950, JWK 651, seen here driven by Bert Hadley, was fitted with a small aero screen, mirror cowl, twin spot lights, lightweight bucket seats and a 25-gallon fuel tank with quick-action filler. *LAT*

40 | Exceptional Cars

Le Mans 24 Hours

- JWK 651 sits in the pits during practice for the 1950 Le Mans 24 Hours. The three Jaguar XK 120s were all works-prepared but privately owned. *LAT*

Works mechanic John Lea (left) with JWK 651, *en route* to Le Mans. Note the full windscreen fitted for the journey, together with rear wheel spats. *JD Classics*

V12 engines, entered by Luigi Chinetti. One was driven by Raymond Sommer and Dorino Serafini, the other by Chinetti himself and 'Heldé' (Pierre Louis-Dreyfus). Two 166 MMs were also entered by Chinetti for Porfirio Rubirosa/Pierre Leygonie and Yvonne Simon/Michel Casse, while a third was entered by Lord Selsdon for himself and Jean Lucas to drive.

Briggs Cunningham entered two 5.4-litre Cadillacs, one that was christened '*Le Monstre*' by the French because of its unlovely but supposedly aerodynamic bodyshell. Cunningham himself and Phil Walters drove '*Le Monstre*', while the other car, a standard Coupe de Ville, was handled by Sam and Miles Collier. Sydney Allard entered a 5.4-litre Cadillac-engined Allard J2 with Tom Cole as co-driver, while Louis Rosier and Pierre Meyrat each had their privately entered 4.5-litre Talbot-Lago T26s, co-driven by Jean-Louis Rosier and Guy Mairesse respectively.

Aston Martin brought three 2.6-litre DB2 cars for George Abecassis/Lance Macklin, Eric Thompson/John Gordon and Reg Parnell/Charles Brackenbury. Gordini had two new T15s with supercharged Simca engines for Maurice Trintignant/Robert Manzon and Juan-Manuel Fangio/José Froilán González, along with two cars in the 1,500cc class for Jean Behra/Roger Loyer and André Simon/Aldo Gordini.

Added to the mix were two Delahayes, one Delage, a pair of Bentleys, a Nash-Healey (with Tony Rolt and Duncan Hamilton at the wheel), a pair of Frazer Nashes, a 4.75-litre supercharged diesel two-stroke MAP, and a 4.4-litre diesel Delettrez. These, together with a variety of Renaults, Monopoles, Panhards and DBs in the smaller classes, comprised the 60 starters, the maximum number permitted, selected from a record entry of 122 cars.

Almost the entire course had been resurfaced since the previous year and Sommer set the fastest time in practice in one of the new Ferrari 195 S models. In those days practice times did not count when it came to setting the grid, the cars instead lined up in order of engine size, the two Allards at the head of the echelon formation in front of the pits in readiness for the traditional Le Mans start.

After a cloudy beginning, the day was bright and sunny by the time of the 4.00pm race start and when the flag fell the drivers sprinted across the road and jumped into their respective machines. *The Autocar* described the scene:

'Then, abruptly, the whole scene sprang to life and the silence was suddenly disrupted; the flag fell, there was the quick scurry of running feet, followed by the slam of doors and the whine of starter motors, with an occasional spitback from a reluctant engine – and the green Allard, driven by Tom Cole, streaked out of the line, and got away to a clear 100-yard lead over the Cadillacs, the MAP-Diesel and the whole howling mob of cars.'

Le Mans 24 Hours

Fangio in his Gordini was delayed at the start with a misfire and Rosier's Talbot was also slow away. After five minutes the cars appeared from Maison Blanche corner, the blue Ferrari of Sommer, who had overtaken a dozen cars, leading at the end of the first lap. He was followed by the Allard of Cole, Meyrat's Talbot, Peter Whitehead's XK 120, Trintignant's Gordini, Hadley in JWK 651, then Haines in the third of the XK 120s.

By lap two, Sommer had pulled out quite a lead over Cole and Meyrat, while on the same lap Cunningham put 'Le Monstre' into the sand bank at Mulsanne and spent 15 minutes digging it out. On the fifth lap, Rosier's Talbot took third from Meyrat and Chinetti in the other big Ferrari moved into fifth.

Sommer continued to set the pace and by the end of the first hour had extended his lead over Cole, who was then overtaken by Rosier, with Meyrat fourth, Chinetti fifth and Trintignant sixth. On lap 19 Sommer broke the circuit record from 1939, lapping at 98.3mph and raised it to 98.88mph three laps later. It was not to last though, and when Sommer had to pit to change a plug, he dropped to fifth and handed the lead to Rosier.

At end of four hours (8pm) Rosier had completed 45 laps and was a lap ahead of the Chinetti/'Heldé' Ferrari, with Sommer and Meyrat on the same lap ahead of Cole and Hadley. Shortly after taking the lead, in the cool evening air, Rosier set a new lap record of 4m 53.5s, a speed of 102.84mph and the first 100mph (160kph) lap at Le Mans.

● Snapshot of JWK 651 at the roadside on its way to the start of the 24 Hours. The full windscreen has been left at the Jaguar team's base and the single aero screen fitted for the race. *Klemantaski Collection/ Louis Klemantaski*

Le Mans 24 Hours

Into the fast lane: JWK 651, with Leslie Johnson at the wheel, accelerates hard at the start of the Mulsanne straight. *LAT*

The Jaguars now made their first stops, with Haines handing over to Clark and Whitehead to Marshall. The latter stop was a long one, with all four wheels being removed in order to adjust the brakes. Johnson took over from Hadley in number 17 Jaguar.

As the evening wore on, more trouble struck the Sommer/Serafini Ferrari, which had to pit with a broken dynamo mounting. The pair eventually retired with no lights or ignition. At midnight, after eight hours of racing, Rosier led Chinetti by two laps, with Meyrat's Talbot third another lap in arrears, Johnson/Hadley fourth, also three laps behind the leader, Allard/Cole fifth, and Rolt/Hamilton sixth.

Towards dawn, patchy mist began to affect the sections around Arnage and Maison Blanche and this did not help the Jaguar drivers, who were finding that their brakes were not as effective as earlier, even though Johnson and Hadley were maintaining fourth place. Meanwhile, the Chinetti/'Heldé' Ferrari dropped back with differential problems and was to retire mid-morning.

After 12 hours (4am), the two Talbots of Rosier/Rosier and Meyrat/Mairesse led, six laps apart, then a lap back was the Jaguar of Johnson/Hadley and the Rolt/Hamilton Nash-Healey. Next up, in fifth place, was the Allard, but this soon had to make an unscheduled pit stop, having lost its two lowest gears; it was jammed into top gear and set off again, now eighth.

Jaguar XK 120 – JWK 651 | 45

Le Mans 24 Hours

Rounding Indianapolis corner, JWK 651 with Bert Hadley at the wheel is followed by 'Le Monstre' – the Briggs Cunningham-entered Cadillac with special 'spyder' bodywork. The car, driven by Cunningham and Phil Walters, spent much of the race jammed in top gear but finished in 11th place. *LAT*

At 5am Louis Rosier pitted and handed over to his son, Jean-Louis, who went out for just two laps. When he returned to the pits a rocker shaft had to be changed, losing five laps, after which Rosier Senior took over again, now in third place. The second Talbot of Meyrat and Mairesse now led for three hours with Johnson and Hadley in JWK 651 in a splendid second place. However, they were hampered by failing brakes, which allowed Rosier to catch and pass them.

At 8am, after 16 hours of racing, Meyrat still led, having completed 171 laps, but Rosiers were only a lap behind, on 170. Johnson/Hadley were also on 170, followed by Rolt/Hamilton another lap behind them. Around this time, Jean Lucas crashed the last remaining Ferrari at Tertre Rouge, bringing to an end a miserable race for the previous year's winning constructor. The Simon/Casse 166 MM had run out of fuel due to a miscalculation early in the race, while the Rubirosa/Leygonie car had retired with clutch problems.

Meanwhile Louis Rosier was on a charge and soon back into the lead despite hitting an owl, which broke the car's windscreen. By 10am the two Talbots were

Night-time pit stop for Leslie Johnson in JWK 651. The car ran in fourth place for most of the night, briefly holding second place early Sunday morning.
Klemantaski Collection/ Louis Klemantaski

running first and second, the Rosiers from Meyrat/Mairesse. The Nash-Healey of Rolt/Hamilton was third, Johnson/Hadley in JWK 651 fourth, followed by the Abecassis/Macklin Aston and the Allard of Allard/Cole. Haines and Clark were eighth in their XK 120, with Whitehead and Marshall 15th. However, the Rolt/Hamilton third place was short-lived for their car was knocked off the track by Henri Louveau's Delage, causing them to lose 45 minutes in the pits for repairs.

At midday, after 20 hours, the two Talbots continued to lead, only a lap apart, Rosier on 215 and Meyrat 214. JWK 651 was still in third, three laps back on 211, and then a lap behind on 210 was the Nash-Healey.

For a long time all of the Jaguar drivers had been having to use heavy engine braking due to their lack of brakes and then, at 1.05pm, with just under three hours to run, the strain took its toll and Johnson had to retire JWK 651 with a broken clutch. *The Autocar* described its demise:

'Suddenly, Johnson's white Jaguar appeared on the run up to the pits travelling very slowly; then it stopped altogether and Johnson got out and pushed, but he was

Le Mans 24 Hours

● A sad end to a good run – JWK 651 abandoned at the side of the track not far from the pits, after Johnson had tried to resuscitate its failed clutch. *LAT*

unable to surmount the slope and stopped just before reaching the pit area, running and walking on himself to his pit. A brief consultation and he trotted back again to work feverishly on the car for some time – but all to no avail, as the clutch refused to grip at all, and to everyone's sorrow the car had to be withdrawn, when firmly in third place with only three hours to go.'

At the front the two Talbots continued to circulate, albeit at reduced pace, while Cole was lapping quickly in the Allard and caught Rolt for third place with half an hour to go. Rolt was nursing the Healey with brake trouble and a problem with the back axle caused by the earlier hit from the Delage.

Louis Rosier led the Talbot one-two across the line, having covered a record distance of 2,153.2 miles. He had driven all but two laps of the gruelling event, in which just 29 out of the original 60 starters made it to the finish. Clark and Haines finished 12th, slowed by an oil leak onto the clutch in the closing stages, while Whitehead and Marshall came in 15th, still suffering from brake problems.

This was highlighted by *The Autocar*, which

Le Mans 24 Hours

Victory at Le Mans in 1950 went to the Talbot-Lago T26 driven by Louis Rosier and his son Jean-Louis. *LAT*

commented that before Jaguar could hope to achieve success in events of this type, research would have to be carried out on the braking system, 'which failed to stand up for so long a period to the loads imposed upon it by their speed and weight'. The magazine concluded:

'Collectively, a lot of trouble experienced by the competing cars was associated with brakes, clutch linings and tyres, emphasising the fast nature of the circuit in its new form. Naturally, when a car is developing difficulties with failing brakes, the driver uses the gear box to the fullest extent as a means of slowing the car for corners, and this extra strain brings in its wake trouble with the clutch and the transmission generally.'

This may have been the case, but 'Lofty' England later told co-author Philip Porter that Johnson was very rough on his cars, and Hadley put the failure down to Johnson practising standing starts before the race.

The significance of the XK 120s' performance should not be under-estimated though. The exercise gave Jaguar the confidence to build the C-type, which went on to win Le Mans the following year and again in 1953.

Jaguar XK 120 – JWK 651 | 49

Le Mans 24 Hours

Hard at work: Leslie Johnson sweeps JWK 651 through the curves with confidence but stopping was a different story, as the car suffered braking problems before clutch failure forced its retirement. *Klemantaski Collection/ Louis Klemantaski*

Results

1	Louis Rosier/Jean-Louis Rosier (4.5-litre Talbot T26GS)	256 laps, 2,153.2 miles (89.73mph)
2	Pierre Meyrat/Guy Mairesse (4.5-litre Talbot MD)	255 laps
3	Sydney Allard/Tom Cole (5.4-litre Allard)	251 laps
4	Tony Rolt/Duncan Hamilton (3.8-litre Nash-Healey)	250 laps
5	George Abecasis/Lance Macklin (2.5-litre Aston Martin DB2)	249 laps
6	Reg Parnell/Charles Brackenbury (2.5-litre Aston Martin DB2)	244 laps
7	Henri Louveau/Jean Estager (3-litre Delage D6)	241 laps
8	Eddie Hall/Tom Clarke (4.5-litre Bentley)	236 laps
9	'Taso' Mathieson/Dickie Stoop (2-litre Frazer Nash)	235 laps
10	Miles Collier/Sam Collier (5.4-litre Cadillac Coupe de Ville)	233 laps

DNF Leslie Johnson/Bert Hadley (Jaguar XK 120)
Fastest lap: Rosier 4m 53.5s (102.84mph) **record**
Index of Performance: 1= Abecassis/Macklin and Jean de Montrémy/Jean Hémard (750cc Monopole)

Herbert Lewis 'Bert' Hadley

Bert Hadley was born in 1910 and became an apprentice with Austin at Longbridge in 1926. He was assigned to the racing team, eventually becoming a works driver.

Hadley's racing career encompassed sprints and hill climbs as well as road racing at circuits such as Crystal Palace. His first outing at Le Mans was in 1937 at the wheel of an Austin Seven, co-driving with Charlie Dodson but the pair failed to finish. They had more success at the Donington 12 Hours that year, coming home seventh, while Hadley also retired from the Brooklands 500km event, again at the wheel of an Austin Seven.

In 1950 Hadley co-drove with Leslie Johnson at Le Mans in JWK 651, the pair retiring from third place with clutch failure. The following year he was at the wheel of a Jowett Jupiter with Charles Goodacre, again retiring, this time early on with electrical problems. His best result of 1951 was at the Tourist Trophy when he finished 17th in the Jowett. Le Mans in 1952, again in the Jowett but this time with Tommy Wisdom, brought another retirement. Hadley was also part of the four-driver team, along with Johnson, Stirling Moss and Jack Fairman, who averaged over 100mph for a week in an XK 120 (669002) at Montlhéry.

For 1953 Hadley returned to his roots and was at the wheel of an Austin-Healey 100 at Le Mans. Partnered with Johnson, he finally achieved a finish, the pair coming home 11th. Earlier in the year, Hadley had retired his Nash-Healey from the Mille Miglia. His last Le Mans came in 1955 when he finished 15th at the wheel of a Triumph TR2 partnered by Ken Richardson.

He died in July 1993.

Bert Hadley pictured at Le Mans in 1955. *Revs Institute for Automotive Research/George Phillips*

Chapter 6
Silverstone One Hour Production Sports Car race
26 August 1950

The former Second World War bomber airfield at Silverstone in Northamptonshire had only opened its doors to motor racing in October 1948, when the first RAC Grand Prix was held there on a track laid out along the perimeter roads and runways. The event was a huge success and was repeated the following year on 14 May. Another Formula 1 race was also held in 1949 on 20 August – the *Daily Express* International Trophy Meeting – and supporting the main event were races for 500cc single-seaters and production sports cars.

In 1950 the International Trophy event was held on 26 August and, due to the large number of entries, the production sports car race was split into two parts, for up to and over 2-litres, with the overall result being decided on time aggregate.

The alloy XK 120s of Leslie Johnson, Nick Haines (to be driven by Tony Rolt), Peter Walker and Tommy Wisdom were entered. A few days beforehand a fifth XK 120, Johnson's winning car from the previous year (HKV 500), was readied with the intention of it being driven by Tazio Nuvolari, at the request of the race organisers, the British Racing Drivers' Club. However, after only a few laps of practice, Nuvolari was taken ill and did not race, his car being taken over by Peter Whitehead. Other notable entries included Duncan Hamilton in a Healey Silverstone, Raymond Sommer and Reg Parnell in Aston Martin DB2s, and Sydney Allard in an Allard J2.

The event for the smaller-engined cars was held earlier in the day and produced a dominant display by the Ferrari 166 MMs of Alberto Ascari, the winner, and second-placed Dorino Serafini.

Between the two races, however, there was a cloudburst. Although the rain had stopped by the time the over 2-litre cars lined up, the track remained damp in places.

Motor Sport reported: 'As the Production cars left from a Le Mans start, Peter Walker led at Club Corner, followed by Rolt and Whitehead, but by lap two Allard had passed Whitehead, whose Jaguar retired before the finish – so perhaps Nuvolari was wise not to drive it.'

Johnson, in JWK 651, had trouble starting his engine and was last away, but was soon catching up when he spun on oil dropped by Whitehead's car, which had lost it oil filter plug. Undeterred, Johnson set off after the field again and eventually finished eighth.

Sommer, in his Aston Martin, was another to be affected by the oil and was passed by the Healey of Hamilton who, try as he might, could not catch the leading Jaguars of Walker and Rolt which, according to *Motor Sport*, 'dominated the race, grandly driven, tyres howling, 1½-2 mph faster than the Healey'.

The overall results were combined with those of the under 2-litre race, with Ascari declared the overall winner from Serafini, with Walker third and Johnson down in 14th. Jaguar, however, won the team prize.

Had the track been dry for the second event, the results might have been even better for the Jaguars.

Johnson had trouble starting the engine of JWK 651 at the One Hour Production Sports Car Race at Silverstone but worked his way through the field to eighth place by the finish, despite spinning on oil dropped by Peter Whitehead's XK 120. *LAT*

Silverstone One Hour Production Sports Car race

- Johnson, in his trademark white overalls and helmet, passes the Silverstone pits, which in those days were located between Abbey and Woodcote corners. *LAT*

- JWK 651 was one of four of the six alloy-bodied competition XK 120s to be entered for the race, the others being those of Nick Haines (driven by Tony Rolt), eventual winner Peter Walker and Tommy Wisdom. *Klemantaski Collection/ Louis Klemantaski*

54 | Exceptional Cars

Silverstone One Hour Production Sports Car race

Johnson finished eighth in the race but 14th on aggregate when the results were combined with those of the under 2-litre event.
Guy Griffiths Collection

Results – Over 2-litre race

1	Peter Walker (Jaguar XK 120)	29 laps in 1h 0m 2.0s (81.88mph)
2	Tony Rolt (Jaguar XK 120)	+14.0s
3	Duncan Hamilton (Healey Silverstone)	
4	Raymond Sommer (Aston Martin DB2)	
5	Sydney Allard (Allard J2)	
6	Reg Parnell (Aston Martin DB2)	
7	Tommy Wisdom (Jaguar XK 120)	
8	**Leslie Johnson (Jaguar XK 120)**	
9	Eric Thompson (Aston Martin DB2)	
10	Ken Watkins (Allard J2)	

Fastest lap: Walker and Rolt, 2m 3.0s

Chapter 7
Tourist Trophy, Dundrod
16 September 1950

The Royal Automobile Club's Tourist Trophy is the oldest trophy still to be awarded in motorsport. It has been contested on various circuits and by a wide range of categories of cars over the years, with winners including Rudolf Caracciola (Mercedes-Benz), Tazio Nuvolari (Alfa Romeo and MG) and Stirling Moss (Jaguar, Mercedes-Benz and Aston Martin).

The race was first held in 1905 on the Highlands Course, when it was won by John Napier driving an Arrol-Johnston, and was then held irregularly until 1928 when it began a nine-year run at the Ards circuit in Northern Ireland before moving in 1937 to Donington in England. Following the Second World War, the venue became Dundrod in Northern Ireland and then Goodwood in 1959. From 1953 to 1964 the Tourist Trophy was a round of the World Sportscar Championship.

The first post-war Tourist Trophy took place on 16 September 1950 on the new 7.4-mile Dundrod circuit, created on public roads closed for the occasion.

This was the race they said Stirling Moss was too young and inexperienced to enter; it was held on the day before his 21st birthday. Despite being in his third full season of racing, none of the manufacturers would provide him with a car.

Unperturbed, Moss persuaded Tommy Wisdom, the motoring correspondent of the *Daily Herald*, to lend him his Jaguar XK 120, JWK 988; for this race Wisdom was driving a Jupiter for the factory Jowett team. Once this was agreed, 'Lofty' England made a standard XK 120 available to Moss prior to the event so that he could become familiar with the car.

Needless to say, Moss proved all his doubters wrong, including Jaguar team leader Leslie Johnson. Moss set the fastest time in dry practice with a lap of 5m 28s, an average speed of 81.39mph, and went on to win despite atrocious weather conditions. In fact it was the weather, and the associated discomfort, that seemed to preoccupy *Motor Sport*'s William Boddy (WB) in his report of the event: 'The press were virtually rendered inoperative, for no press box was provided and the press tent eventually blew over – after which drenched pressmen had to wait for a prodigious time for the final results and were summarily ordered out of his caravan by the press officer. Incidentally, the race bulletins had a great many typing errors…'

The temporary nature of the track, with scaffolding and canvas grandstands which proved totally inadequate for the conditions, also came in for criticism.

The race, which was run as a handicap based on engine capacity, failed to attract overseas entries such as Alfa Romeo, Ferrari and Talbot-Lago, and instead the entry was dominated by British sports cars: Allard, Aston Martin, Frazer Nash, Healey, HRG, Jaguar, Jowett and MG.

With Moss entered by Wisdom, Jaguar was officially represented by Johnson (in JWK 651), Peter Whitehead and Nick Haines, but Haines crashed in practice and was unable to start. Bob Gerard was in his Frazer Nash Le Mans Replica, with Norman Culpan and Tony Crook in their 'High Speed' models. Aston Martin fielded three DB2s for Reg Parnell, George Abecassis and Lance Macklin, while Sydney Allard, Guy Warburton and Ken Watkins were behind the wheels of a trio of Allard J2s.

Competitors in the RAC Tourist Trophy at Dundrod faced torrential rain and gale-force winds, as can be seen in this photograph of JWK 651 during the event. *LAT*

Tourist Trophy, Dundrod

Johnson, in JWK 651, gets away first at the start of the 1950 RAC Tourist Trophy, flanked by the other XK 120s of Peter Whitehead (5) and eventual winner Stirling Moss (7).
Philip Porter archive

Heavy rain and strong winds greeted the 31 starters as they lined up for the 2.00pm start, the race scheduled to run for three hours. The flag was dropped by Sir Basil Brooke, Prime Minister of Northern Ireland, and Johnson was first away in JWK 651, followed by Ken Watkins's Allard, Moss's Jaguar, Warburton's Allard and Macklin's Aston Martin. At Leathemstown Corner, part way round the lap, the order was Johnson with Moss right on his tail, followed by Parnell, Watkins, Whitehead, Macklin and Abecassis, but by the end of the lap Allard had stormed into third place and Whitehead had taken Watkins for fifth.

With just 15 minutes of the race run, Walter Freed crashed his Healey Silverstone into a post at Ireland's Corner, while 'T Flack' hit a tree with his MG but continued, neither driver being injured. On the second lap, Moss passed Johnson to take the lead, with Allard still in third ahead of Whitehead and Macklin. Allard was caught out by the terrible conditions and he went off into a field at the hairpin. The car was pushed back on by spectators and Allard pitted to have it checked over. It was soon back in again for the offside wheel to be changed. By now the gearbox was jammed in second, preventing Allard from putting up any further challenge to the flying Jaguars.

After half an hour, Moss, who had put in a lap at

Tourist Trophy, Dundrod

Stirling Moss, driving Tommy Wisdom's XK 120 (JWK 988), followed Johnson in JWK 651 for the first lap before taking the lead and pulling away to an impressive victory in appalling conditions. *LAT*

76.5mph, still led Johnson with Culpan's Frazer Nash now in third ahead of Whitehead and Parnell. Wisdom must have pondered over his decision to race the Jupiter instead of his own XK when he had to retire with a blown gasket. Johnson, meanwhile, under pressure from Whitehead, skidded at Quarry Corner.

The rain was reducing visibility and mist obscured the high parts of the circuit, making driving conditions ever more treacherous. *Motor Sport* reported that 'at Ireland's Corner the only remaining spectators were a lady and gentleman and small boy under a large umbrella'. It was worse for the open cars, such as the Jaguars, while at least the closed Astons afforded their occupants some shelter. The only advantage of the conditions was that tyre wear proved to be much less than expected, allowing the Jaguars to run through without stopping.

At the two-hour mark Moss still led but Whitehead had passed Johnson for second, and was 27 seconds ahead of his team-mate but 1m 59s behind Moss. Culpan's Frazer Nash was next, the nearest rival to the seemingly dominant Jaguars.

As the race wore on the weather deteriorated still further, and the wind threatened to blow down the flimsy pits. At 4.30pm, after two and a half hours of driving, Moss still led but Culpan had slowed up in the

Tourist Trophy, Dundrod

- After initially being refused an entry for the event due to being too young and inexperienced, Stirling Moss put on a magnificent display of wet-weather driving in Tommy Wisdom's alloy-bodied XK 120. Here he sweeps past the MG TD of 'T Flack', which finished 23rd. *LAT*

The fine weather tells us that this photograph must have been taken during practice for the 1950 RAC Tourist Trophy. Despite leading for the first lap, Johnson experienced brake problems and eventually finished third on the road but seventh on handicap. *LAT*

Frazer Nash and dropped back to sixth, while Johnson, who was suffering from brake problems, still lay third on the road, but was down to seventh on handicap, behind the Astons of Parnell and Abecassis.

Towards the end, Moss was given the 'slow' signal from the pits by his father but then concern grew that Gerard, who had hauled his Frazer Nash up into third, might be ahead on handicap. On the last lap, Moss was therefore given the 'flat out' signal and he responded with a lap at an average speed of 77.61mph, a record for the track.

He took the rather sodden chequered flag, ahead of Whitehead and Gerard, followed by Parnell, Abecassis and Culpan. Johnson's seventh place on handicap, while disappointing given his early pace, was still enough for Jaguar to take the team prize. And Moss was able to start celebrating his 21st birthday early.

Results

1	Stirling Moss (Jaguar XK 120)	3h 00m 00s, 225.452 miles (75.15mph)
2	Peter Whitehead (Jaguar XK 120)	222.392 miles
3	Bob Gerard (Frazer Nash Le Mans Replica)	215.770 miles
4	Reg Parnell (Aston Martin DB2)	217.168 miles
5	George Abecassis (Aston Martin DB2)	217.148 miles
6	Norman Culpan (Frazer Nash High Speed)	213.452 miles
7	**Leslie Johnson (Jaguar XK 120)**	**219.180 miles**
8	Lance Macklin (Aston Martin DB2)	215.354 miles
9	Ernie Wilkinson (Healey Silverstone)	211.791 miles
10	Tony Crook (Frazer Nash High Speed)	207.739 miles

Fastest lap: Moss (77.61mph)
Team award: Jaguar – Moss, Whitehead, Johnson

Chapter 8
Records at Montlhéry
1950 and 1951

The Autodrome de Linas-Montlhéry, just outside Paris, was opened in October 1924 and comprised a 1.583-mile (2.548km) banked oval that quickly became the scene of many record-breaking attempts. The following year a road course was completed that incorporated one of the banked turns and measured 7.76 miles (12.5km) in length.

The first race at Montlhéry was the French Grand Prix on 26 July 1925, won by Robert Benoist in a Delage. The event returned in 1927 and continued to be held there from 1931 to 1937. The track was abandoned during the Second World War and fell into a state of disrepair but was subsequently renovated and part of it converted for use as a vehicle proving ground. It was also the venue for the 1,000km de Paris, which ran irregularly from 1956 to 2004.

In October 1950, Leslie Johnson, partnered by Stirling Moss, took JWK 651 to the banked track of Montlhéry with the intention of averaging 100mph for 24 hours. The pair each did three-hour stints of driving and achieved an average speed of 107.46mph, covering 2,570.16 miles. During the final hour they averaged 112mph with a best lap at 126.2mph. It was the first time a production car had averaged over 100mph for 24 hours.

Motor Sport reported: 'During the evening of October 25th Leslie Johnson's well-known white XK 120 Jaguar completed a 24-hour run at Montlhéry during which it averaged 107.46mph. Stirling Moss acted as co-driver, 122.4 miles were covered in the 24th hour and several laps were put in at 126mph. During the run it was dark for thirteen hours, but no track lighting was employed, Johnson and Moss relying on the standard Lucas lighting on the car. This is a very fine demonstration of Jaguar reliability-cum-speed, and it seems very unselfish of a private owner to have submitted his car to it. This, and the TT victory, have re-established the warmest admiration for the XK 120 amongst even the most cynical, but if any similar achievement is contemplated, let it be an attack on those Belgian sprint records which Jaguar propose to win back from Lycett's 8-litre Bentley and Tyrer's 2-litre BMW.'

In an interview in 2012, Moss said that JWK 651 was his favourite classic Jaguar of all time. 'That was the first time that a production car had driven for 24 hours at an average of more than 100mph,' he said. 'We swapped drivers every three hours, travelling over 2,500 miles with a fastest lap of 125mph. The track was tough on the car, but the XK 120 held out – that's why it's my favourite Jaguar.'

In the December 1950 issue of *Motor Sport*, Jaguar took a full-page advertisement, the headline of which read: '107mph for 24 Hours.' It went on: 'Jaguar Cars congratulate Mr Leslie Johnson, whose privately owned Jaguar XK 120 driven by himself and Mr Stirling Moss completed 24 hours' continuous running, at an average speed of 107.46 mph at Montlhéry, October 24/25 1950. In the last hour, an average speed of 112.40mph was actually attained. Following such successes as the Alpine Trial, Silverstone and the Tourist Trophy, this latest achievement again proves Jaguar's outstanding capacity for sustained high speed and reliability.'

In March 1951, Johnson returned to the same circuit and, driving solo, averaged 131.83mph for one hour,

Stirling Moss at the wheel of JWK 651 in October 1950 at the Autodrome de Linas-Montlhéry. Over a 24-hour period, he and Leslie Johnson averaged a speed of 107.46mph, covering a distance of 2,570.16 miles. It seems likely that the car did the actual record-breaking run with these dark-coloured wheels and a single aeroscreen fitted.
Philip Porter Archive

Records at Montlhéry

with a fastest lap at 134.43mph. It was a remarkable achievement for the period, bearing in mind this was a production sports car with 1940s technology, including leaf-spring rear suspension and narrow cross-ply tyres, while the track, with its 30-degree banking, was excessively rough. Johnson said afterwards that the car felt so good it could have gone on for a week.

- During the final hour of the record-breaking 24-hour run, Moss and Johnson averaged 112mph and set a fastest lap at 126.2mph. It was the first time that a production car had averaged over 100mph for 24 hours.
  Jaguar Heritage Trust

107 M.P.H FOR 24 HOURS

Officially observed and timed by the Automobile Club de France.

Jaguar Cars congratulate Mr. Leslie Johnson, whose privately owned Jaguar XK 120 driven by himself and Mr. Stirling Moss completed 24 hours' continuous running, at an average speed of 107.46 m.p.h. at Montlhery, October 24/25, 1950. In the last hour, an average speed of 112.40 m.p.h. was actually attained. Following such successes as the Alpine Trial, Silverstone and the Tourist Trophy, this latest achievement again proves Jaguar's outstanding capacity for sustained high speed and reliability.

Another phenomenal **JAGUAR** *success!*

- Pit stop – Johnson and Moss changed over every three hours during the course of the 24-hour run.
  Philip Porter archive

Records at Montlhéry

● The successful team behind the record-breaking run stand proudly with JWK 651.
Paul Skilleter photo archive

● Johnson returned to Montlhéry in 1951, this time driving solo, and set a record speed of 131.83mph for one hour, including a fastest lap at 134.43mph.
Paul Skilleter photo archive

Stirling Moss

Stirling Moss at the wheel of JWK 651 at Montlhéry in October 1950. He became a Jaguar works driver the following year.
Philip Porter archive

The fabulous career of Stirling Moss has already been well-documented, so for the purpose of this book we will confine ourselves mainly to his exploits with Jaguar.

Moss bought a Cooper-JAP 500cc car in 1948 and won his first race that year at Brough Aerodrome. His big break came in 1950 at Dundrod when Tommy Wisdom lent him his alloy XK 120 (660057) in which, on the eve of his 21st birthday, Moss won the RAC Tourist Trophy, an event he was to win on a further six occasions. This led to Moss partnering Leslie Johnson at Montlhéry in JWK 651 in October, when the pair averaged over 100mph for 24 hours (see the preceding pages for accounts of both occasions).

Moss was a works Jaguar driver for 1951 and was part of a two-car team, again with Johnson, that tackled the Mille Miglia in XK 120s, but both Jaguars were caught up in a multi-car accident only a few miles from the start.

Moss's next outing was at the *Daily Express* International Trophy meeting at Silverstone, where he won the Production Sports Car Race in one of the first steel-bodied XK 120s ahead of the similar cars of Charlie Dodson and Leslie Johnson. At Le Mans, Moss raced one of the new C-type Jaguars (XKC 002), partnered by Jack Fairman, and the pair were leading when, at around midnight, a broken con-rod caused their retirement. In September Moss was back at Dundrod, the scene of his victory the previous year, for the Tourist Trophy, driving the same C-type that he had used at Le Mans. He took an easy win ahead of team-mate Peter Walker and then, to cap it off, later the same month he drove the C-type to victory at Goodwood in both the sports car and handicap events.

Moss kicked off his 1952 season with Jaguar in the Lyons-Charbonnières rally, finishing second in class in his own XK 120. Then at Goodwood he drove a C-type fitted with newly developed disc brakes and finished fourth in the Easter Handicap. He and Jaguar's test driver, Norman Dewis, retired from that year's Mille Miglia but the Silverstone International meeting brought more success, Moss winning three times in Jaguars. He took a Mark VII saloon to victory in the Touring Car Race, won the Production Sports Car Race in a C-type, and then won a novelty 'International Race of Champions' for six standard XK 120s ahead of Baron 'Toulo' de Graffenreid.

The Monaco Grand Prix in 1952 was held for sports cars and Moss was entered in a C-type, but he was disqualified for receiving outside assistance after sliding off on oil. Le Mans that year did not bring any more success, his C-type retiring with overheating problems. The sports car race at Reims, however, brought more luck and Moss took his C-type to victory, the first international win for a car equipped with disc brakes. Another victory in the C-type came at Boreham in a 100-mile sports car race and then he was back at Montlhéry for a seven-day record attempt with an XK 120 Fixed Head Coupé. At the Goodwood 9 Hours in August a long delay in the pits with rear axle problems meant that fifth place was all he and Walker could manage in their C-type. Moss won a sports car event at Turnberry a week later, followed by second places at Goodwood's September meeting and at Charterhall. In November he entered the *Daily Express* Rally, driving his own XK 120 Fixed Head Coupé, and finished 13th.

Moss had taken delivery of this XK 120 earlier in the year and specified it with left-hand drive as he intended to use it mainly on the continent. He also planned to use the car to tow a luxury caravan in order to save on hotel bills as he travelled around Europe. *Motor Sport* reported: 'In order to fulfil his many engagements in

Moss took delivery of a Jaguar XK 120 Fixed Head Coupé in 1952 with the intention of using it to travel to continental races towing a luxury caravan.
Getty Images/Hulton Archive

Stirling Moss

- Moss won the Tourist Trophy at Dundrod for the second time in 1951, driving the works Jaguar C-type (XKC 002). He took the lead on the opening lap and stayed there to the finish. *LAT*

Continental races in 1952, Stirling Moss has ordered a Jaguar XK 120 coupe, which is to be fitted with a special tow bar attachment for drawing the caravan which will serve as living quarters for himself and his manager [Ken Gregory]. Car and van are to be delivered on the Continent and will remain there during the whole season. The complete equipe will be painted in Moss's personal racing colours – cream and green.'

Unfortunately, while going down a steep hill on their way to Luxembourg, the caravan broke free from the XK 120 while Gregory was driving. Realising what had happened, he accelerated hard to try to outrun the careering caravan but it overtook them and crashed into a concrete kilometre stone, coming to rest, smashed, in the middle of the road.

For 1953 Moss was once again behind the wheel of a C-type in the Mille Miglia but retired with a broken rear axle. He won the Saloon Car Race at Silverstone in May in a Mark VII but could only manage seventh in the Sports Car event in his C-type. For Le Mans, Moss was partnered by Walker and after being delayed by a blocked fuel filter, the pair took their C-type to second place behind team-mates Tony Rolt and Duncan Hamilton. The British Empire Trophy at Douglas, Isle of Man, resulted in second place in heat three and fourth in the final for Moss, again in the C-type. Then came the

Stirling Moss

> *Moss continued to drive for Jaguar until he was offered a contract by Mercedes-Benz for the 1955 season*

Reims 12 Hours, which produced a magnificent victory for Moss and Peter Whitehead. Moss was runner-up in the C-type at Lisbon in the Jubilee Grand Prix in July but retired from the Goodwood 9 Hours in August. Back at Dundrod for the Tourist Trophy the following month, he won his class and was fourth overall, despite waiting to push his car over the line in order to be classified as a finisher after the rear axle broke three laps from home.

In 1954 Moss campaigned his own Maserati 250F in Formula 1 but still won the Production Touring Car event at May's Silverstone International Trophy meeting in a Mark VII. He drove a works D-type at Le Mans, partnered once more by Walker, but retired with brake trouble. At the Reims 12 Hours a broken drive-shaft sidelined the pair's D-type, while they only managed 18th at that year's Tourist Trophy after rear axle problems.

Moss left the Jaguar fold when he was offered the chance to drive for Mercedes-Benz in 1955. He won the Mille Miglia partnered by Denis Jenkinson, and the British Grand Prix at Aintree, leading home team-mate Juan Manuel Fangio. He was back in a Maserati 250F for 1956, winning in Monaco and Italy, and in 1957 he won the British GP again, after taking over team-mate Tony Brooks's Vanwall.

In 1958 Moss gave the Cooper Car Company its first-ever Formula 1 victory when he took Rob Walker's Climax-engined T43 to victory at the Argentine Grand Prix. For most of that year he again drove for Vanwall, winning the Dutch, Portuguese and Moroccan Grands Prix, and finished just one point behind Mike Hawthorn in the World Championship.

Moss was runner-up to the Formula 1 World Champion again in 1959, driving Walker's Cooper and occasionally a BRM. In sports cars he raced for Aston Martin, which won the World Sports Car Championship.

In 1960, driving Rob Walker's Lotus 18, he took victory at the Monaco Grand Prix, a feat he repeated the following year.

Moss's front-line career ended in 1962 after a heavy crash in a Lotus at Goodwood on 23 April.

Stirling Moss was knighted in 2000 'for services to motor racing'.

At Le Mans in 1954 with the D-type, shared with Peter Walker – it retired with brake failure. Moss drove the D-type in only three races, without much success. *The Revs Institute for Automotive Research/ George Phillips*

Chapter 9
Mille Miglia
29 April 1951

Encouraged by his fifth placing the previous year, Leslie Johnson returned to tackle the Mille Miglia in JWK 651 on 29 April 1951, again with John Lea as his co-driver.

The route had altered slightly from the previous year. It more or less kept to the same roads from the start at Brescia all the way to Rome, except for a diversion between Ravenna and Rimini, via Forli, and a different road between Riete and Rome. From Rome, however, the route now went inland via Viterbo, Siena and Florence, making it 46 miles shorter than the previous route at a mere 978 miles.

The number of entries was down slightly, so that 322 cars left the starting ramp at Brescia, commencing with the first cars in the production class at 9pm on the Saturday. As usual, cars set off at one-minute intervals in classes, with the starting number decided by ballot.

Jaguar was represented by a two-car team of XK 120s, for Johnson and Stirling Moss. Ferrari had 26 cars entered, most of them privately run *Tipo* 166s, but the works brought along four new *Tipo* 340s with 4.1-litre V12 engines, three of them Touring *barchettas* for Alberto Ascari, Dorino Serafini and Vittorio Marzotto, the fourth a Vignale *berlinetta* sports tourer for Luigi Villoresi, who had requested a roof over his head! The previous year's winner, Giannino Marzotto, had put his own bodywork on a Ferrari 212 chassis, a move that apparently did not endear him to Enzo Ferrari.

Alfa Romeo entered an old 412 Spider for Felice Bonetto and two 6C 2500 *berlinettas* for Franco Rol and the Bornigia brothers, Mario and Franco. Lancia fielded six new 2-litre Aurelia B20s including one driven by Giovanni Bracco and Umberto Maglioli. Other notable entries included Tommy Wisdom in an Aston Martin DB2, Donald and Geoffrey Healey in a Nash-Healey, Sydney Allard in his Allard J2, and Franco Cortese in a Frazer Nash Le Mans Replica.

One of the more unusual entries was Clemente Biondetti in a 'Jaguar Special'. This utilised the engine, transmission and suspension from an XK 120, mounted in what one report described as a 'light Italian tubular chassis' and others as a Ferrari chassis.

As the fast sports cars came to the line in the early hours of Sunday morning, Brescia was hit by torrential rain. Just after 4am, and within only 15 miles (or 16, depending on reports) of the start, Ascari, Johnson and Moss were all out. Accounts of the exact circumstances vary slightly. *The Autocar* reported:

'Only 16 miles from the start Ascari, in an open 4,080cc Ferrari, skidded into some parked cars at a bend and bounced into the crowd, two of whom were seriously hurt. Within a few minutes Johnson and Stirling Moss, in Jaguars, and Santori (Alfa) all piled up at the same spot. The crews were unhurt but the cars were out. Johnson had split his fuel tank; Moss continued but a damaged transmission forced his early retirement. Both had found their brakes inoperative when approaching the corner and were convinced that there was oil on the road, but Ferraris blamed mud.'

The Motor, on the other hand, stated:

'A 2-litre car had dropped its oil all over a corner (naturally) and first Moss (Jaguar) and then Johnson (Jaguar) spun like tops out of the race. Next Ascari (4.1-litre Ferrari) slid widely, took the escape road and

Leslie Johnson and his co-driver John Lea in JWK 651 follow team-mates Stirling Moss and Frank Rainbow to scrutineering at the 1951 Mille Miglia. *Archivio Novafoto-Sorlini/ Giorgio Nada Editore*

Mille Miglia

Jaguar entered a two-car team for the 1951 Mille Miglia with Leslie Johnson and John Lea in JWK 651 (left) and Stirling Moss and Frank Rainbow in HKV 500. Both cars were eliminated early in the event when they hit the same patch of oil and crashed out.
Jaguar Heritage Trust

there crashed into a parked car, killing its occupant.'

The version from *Autosport* read:

'Then, on the winding road between Lonato and Dezenzano, near Lake Garda, Ascari's Ferrari struck a patch of oil deposited on a bend by one of the 2-litre class cars which passed through earlier. Ascari skied helplessly off the road into a crowd of spectators, one of whom was killed and others injured. Ascari and his co-driver were unhurt, but the Ferrari was wrecked. Close behind, Stirling Moss and Leslie Johnson (Jaguars) both hit the same oil patch, and were eliminated, which was bad luck indeed.'

The discrepancies show how careful one must be in relying on contemporary reports, especially for a race like the Mille Miglia where few journalists were ever able to witness incidents first-hand. Piecing the information together, it does seem likely that Ascari was the first to leave the road, followed by Moss and Johnson. Ascari later said that he was unsighted due to the headlights of spectators' cars shining on to the road so that competitors' race numbers could be read.

Not long afterwards, Sydney Allard skidded into a mile post and bent the axle on his Allard, while Biondetti had to retire his Jaguar Special when its flexing chassis caused the fan to cut through a radiator hose.

Meanwhile, the previous year's winner, Giannino Marzotto, was setting the pace in his modified Ferrari. At the first control at Ravenna, 190 miles from the start, he was five minutes ahead of Villoresi, who was finding the extra power of his car hard to handle in the conditions, while Serafini was third in his Ferrari. At Senigallia, Marzotto, on hearing a rhythmic thumping noise from the back of the car, stopped with what he thought was a broken rear axle, but later found to be only a thrown tread on a tyre, meaning that he had retired unnecessarily. Serafini was now up to second, four minutes behind Villoresi, but just before Pescara his Ferrari went off the road, up a bank and through trees before dropping into a field, leaving Serafini with a broken arm and leg.

At Pescara, Villoresi led Bracco's Lancia with the remarkable little 1,100cc OSCA of Franco Bordoni in third. When Vittorio Marzotto retired the third of the 4.1-litre Ferraris at Fano, Villoresi's was the only works Ferrari left. He had been off the road twice, damaging the front bodywork, but at Rome, 564 miles into the race and after seven hours 18 minutes of driving, he led at an average speed of just under 80mph. Next up were Bracco/Maglioli in their Lancia, ahead of the Alfa of the Bornigias, who had overtaken Bordoni for third place.

According to *The Autocar*, the section from Rome to Bolsena and then to Radicofani and on to Siena was extremely tiring for the drivers, due to intermittent rain and heavy traffic, 'fortunately most of the latter going in the same direction as the race'! Gearbox problems had left Villoresi with only fourth gear but, nevertheless, at Florence he was two minutes ahead of Bracco/Maglioli with Bordoni third. However, a stop to replace a fuel pump dropped Bordoni's OSCA to 10th.

Mille Miglia

'Just 15 miles from the start, Johnson and Moss were out, both hitting the same oil patch'

The number on the car tells us that Johnson and Lea are about to set off at 4.29am on the 1951 Mille Miglia, in heavy rain.
Archivio Novafoto-Sorlini/ Giorgio Nada Editore

After Florence came the Raticosa and Futa passes. This stretch proved to be the undoing of the Bornigia brothers, whose Alfa went over the edge on the Futa, where there were no retaining walls, and fell 60 feet. The car landed on its wheels but Mario Bornigias fractured his pelvis. This left the Ferrari of Piero Scotti and Amos Ruspaggiari third.

The weather had cleared by the time the crews reached Brescia and Luigi Villoresi and co-driver Piero Cassani were greeted with brilliant sunshine. Between Florence and Brescia Villoresi had been able to extend his lead and took victory by just under 20 minutes from Bracco and Maglioli, whose second place driving a standard 2-litre Lancia was the surprise of the event. Third was Scotti with Paolo Marzotto fourth in his Ferrari 166.

Results

1	405	Luigi Villoresi/Piero Cassani (Ferrari 340 America Berlinette Vignale)	12h 50m 18.0s (75.70mph)
2	332	Giovanni Bracco/Umberto Maglioli (Lancia Aurelia B20)	13h 10m 14.0s
3	434	Piero Scotti/Amos Ruspaggiari (Ferrari 212 Export spider Motto)	13h 22m 04.4s
4	357	Paolo Marzotto/Marino Marini (Ferrari 166 MM Barchetta Touring)	13h 30m 48.0s
5	315	'Ippocampo' (Umberto Castiglioni)/Nando Mori (Lancia Aurelia B20)	13h 47m 30.0s
6	427	Felica Bonetto/Luigi Casnaghi (Alfa Romeo 412 Spider Vignale)	13h 49m 35.s
7	334	Gino Valenzano/Luigi Maggio (Lancia Aurelia B20)	13h 50m 0.0s
8	243	Luigi Fagioli/Vincenzo Borghi (OSCA MT4 1100)	13h 52m 35.0s
9	352	Franco Cortese/Luigi Tagni (Frazer Nash Le Mans Replica)	14h 06m 28.0s
10	242	Franco Bordoni/Cetti Serbelloni (OSCA MT4 1100)	14h 06m 49.0s
DNF	**429**	**Leslie Johnson/John Lea (Jaguar XK 120)**	

Chapter 10
RAC Rally of Great Britain
31 March – 5 April 1952

The RAC Rally was first held in 1932 with 241 competitors starting from nine different locations – London, Bath, Norwich, Leamington, Buxton, Harrogate, Liverpool, Newcastle upon Tyne and Edinburgh – and following different routes, each about 1,000 miles in length, before converging on Torquay. The following year, Hastings was the finish point and the rally ran annually until the outbreak of war, after which it resumed in 1951.

About 250 cars entered the second RAC International Car Rally in 1952, run from 31 March to 5 April. We can only say 'about' because *Motor* gave 249, *The Autocar* 250, *Motor Sport* and *Autosport* 251, and the BBC 252. The 1,800-mile rally started from both Hastings and Scarborough, the two routes converging at Silverstone before heading for Bridport, then through Wales to Blackpool and thence up into Scotland before turning south again to finish at Scarborough four days later.

Autosport reported that by the first evening the exact number of competitors 'remained a little obscure' as there were five non-starters at Scarborough and four at Hastings, but if the total entry was taken as 251, the number that departed still left two cars unaccounted for, so it appears that the final figure was either 240 or 241. What we can be certain of is that there was a strong contingent of XK 120s, including Leslie Johnson in JWK 651 and Ian Appleyard in NUB 120.

Competitors starting from Scarborough set off at 7.30am on Monday 31 March, with those from Hastings scheduled for half an hour later at 8am. However, because of heavy snow over the south of England during the preceding weekend, many of the Hastings starters found it difficult even to reach the start point and sleet was still falling when they did depart.

Old footage from British Pathé shows the cars, including the Cadillac-engined Allard of eventual winner Godfrey Imhof, lined up waiting to be released by the Mayor and Mayoress of Hastings, with a stiff wind blowing across a soaking wet promenade. Later footage shows the snow-covered roads in the surrounding countryside and competitors encountered further delays as conditions worsened from London onwards.

When they did arrive at Silverstone, it was to discover that the scheduled speed test on the new 1.7-mile Club circuit had been cancelled because the track was awash with slush. It was a decision that did not sit well with the competitors, since it had been taken early in the morning and the track was virtually clear by 1pm as the cars arrived.

After leaving Silverstone, the Rally went to Bridport, Dorset, and then to Castle Combe, Wiltshire, where a special timed test of manoeuvring was held in the dark. This did not suit the XKs and none figured in the results. Competitors then headed into the mountains of Wales, with a speed test at Eppynt just before 7am. This was running about three quarters of an hour late due to a problem with the Army radio telephone system between the start and finish lines. According to *Autosport*, many competitors described the test as 'highly dangerous' and 'even experienced drivers such as Leslie Johnson were somewhat shaken by the hazards of the Eppynt test…' Miss Lorna Snow in an XK 120 went off and Johnson, who started JWK 651 a short time after her, was baulked and had to return for

Leslie Johnson, driving JWK 651, lost out on a possible third place on the 1952 RAC Rally of Great Britain due to being penalised for not having rear wheel spats fitted. *LAT*

RAC Rally of Great Britain

● Heavy snow across southern England made conditions difficult for those competitors starting from Hastings, including Johnson in JWK 651. *LAT*

a rerun, which he achieved in the impressive time of 2m 30.4s. Ian Appleyard managed 2m 31.2s, followed by Tom Christie and Jack Broadhead, also in XK 120s.

The cars then headed 120 miles to Blackpool for a series of tests on the promenade, with Imhof's Allard and the XKs of J. Neilson and Appleyard topping the list, each with a time of 19.0 seconds, and Johnson lying sixth with 19.8 seconds.

After an overnight stop at Blackpool, the remaining 225 competitors set off again on the Wednesday morning for the Lake District. At the Hardknott Pass, JWK 651 got stuck in first gear but Johnson not only completed the test using the one gear but also drove on to the next one at Alston. Here, he managed to get second gear working and, using just this and first, reached Edinburgh where the problem was fixed. *Autosport* reported: 'First excitement came from Leslie Johnson (Jaguar) who came screaming into the control just on time. Apparently the day's tests had made the car's gearbox turn stubborn and awkward to the extent of a large portion of the route having to be covered in bottom gear and resulting in a rapid bit of major repairing.' Ian Appleyard, apparently, 'had no complaints to make, having thoroughly enjoyed the day's motoring'.

Parc fermé for the overnight stop was at the

RAC Rally of Great Britain

At one point Johnson was stuck in first gear but still managed to complete the test and was able to fix the problem. *LAT*

Murrayfield rugby stadium and at this stage 217 cars were still running, the leader in the class for open-top cars being Ken Bancroft's Morgan, followed by Appleyard.

At 7am on Thursday the competitors set off for Rest-and-be-Thankful for a speed hill climb where, according to *Autosport*, 'the XK 120s had it mostly their own way'. It reported: 'Leslie Johnson (Jaguar) made spectators pay some real attention. The Jag had definitely recovered from its mileage in bottom gear and went spanking up the hill to cross the line in 72.6s.' But then… 'Ian Appleyard was off like a streak and appeared only as a blur on the road till he reached Stone Bridge. From there he tapered off a little, but bettered Leslie Johnson's time by a second to clock BTD at 71.6s.'

The leading times were Ian Appleyard on 71.6 seconds, Leslie Johnson 72.6 seconds, Jack Broadhead 74.0 seconds, Tom Christie 74.2 seconds and Godfrey Imhof 74.6 seconds. Overall, Bancroft was still leading the open class in his Morgan, ahead of Appleyard.

The route continued through Scotland to Onich, back to Pitlochry, through Kenmore and over the pass at Amulree, where disgruntled local landowners had thrown boulders on to the course, causing considerable damage to some cars. The next control was at Kendal, with just 117 miles left to the finish at Scarborough.

RAC Rally of Great Britain

RAC officials were checking that no competitor averaged more than 40mph on this final section to rally headquarters at the Grand Hotel, where the cars went into overnight *parc fermé* once more. At this point Johnson was penalised 40 marks by the scrutineer at the finish for having no wheel spats fitted on his car. The newly announced wire-wheeled XK 120 Special Equipment model did not have spats, but JWK 651 was not fitted with wire wheels and the officials interpreted the small print accordingly.

Johnson protested but his arguments fell on deaf ears. According to *Autosport*: 'Johnson maintained that he had never had any, and that some XKs were indeed made without them; but his car appeared to have provision for attaching these embellishments and, after appropriate consultation, the Stewards announced regretfully their inability to uphold the protest. It is unfortunate that this question was not ventilated during his initial scrutineering at Hastings.'

The 36 leading drivers were then selected for a speed-regularity test on Oliver's Mount the following morning which was run 'with lengthy and irregular intervals' and a lack of marshals. According to *Autosport*, Imhof 'made the truly perfect run' but 'Leslie Johnson was steady and fast, but this proved to be a practice run, for he appeared again, just as steady and faster still, in what was later announced to be the

● At Rest-and-be-Thankful hill climb the XK 120s had it mostly their own way, with Johnson in particular catching attention with his spectacular driving. *LAT*

● The third-placed XK 120 of Ian Appleyard fitted with its rear wheel spats; the omission of these on JWK 651 caused Johnson to be penalised. *LAT*

78 | Exceptional Cars

RAC Rally of Great Britain

The winner of the 1952 RAC Rally of Great Britain was Godfrey Imhof in his Cadillac-engined Allard. *LAT*

quickest run of the day.' It was to no avail though, for the rejection of his protest meant that his possible third place became 16th.

The Times reported the final day's activity in more detail:

'The deciding factor in the rally was the speed and regularity contest held today on the Oliver's Mount racing circuit, which proved admirable for the purpose. The circuit was divided into two timed sections separated by a neutral zone. The object was to record as nearly as possible identical times for both sections at the best possible speed. The drivers' task was made more difficult by their having to travel without the guidance and help of their passengers in time-keeping.

'The slower of the two sections was mostly uphill with some sharp corners, and it was here that the superior acceleration of the winning Allard and several Jaguars gave them an advantage over the smaller Morgans, which up to this point were favourably placed – partly because they, in turn, had been more suited to the early manoeuvring tests.

'Imhof, who was lying fifth on arriving at Scarborough, gave a superb display of driving skill and time-keeping in covering the two sections in 59.8sec and 59sec, the fastest average of the day, which put him ahead of the favourite, I Appleyard (Jaguar) who was slightly slower. L Johnson (Jaguar) actually did the fastest time, 59.6sec, in the first section, followed by 60.6sec in the second, and this would have given him third place in the open car class had he not lost 40 marks for removing the rear wheel spats on his car. Becquart, who was lying fifth in the closed car cars under 2½ litres class before the final rest, pulled up to first place by making the quickest times, 73.4sec and 72.2sec in the class.'

As rain began to fall it all came to an end and when the results were posted, Godfrey Imhof in his Allard-Cadillac was confirmed as the winner of the open car class, ahead of the XK 120s of Broadhead and Appleyard. An advertisement in *Autosport* the following week proclaimed that Jaguar had finished second, third and fourth, and achieved the best performance by a lady, all in the open car class, during the second RAC International Rally of Great Britain.

Results

Class 1 (Open cars):

1	Godfrey Imhof (Allard)	183.8 marks
2	Jack Broadhead (Jaguar)	185
3	Ian Appleyard (Jaguar)	186.6
4	Tom Christie (Jaguar)	190.8
5	Peter Reece (Morgan)	198.2
6	Peter Morgan (Morgan)	199.4
16	**Leslie Johnson (Jaguar)**	

Class 2 (Closed cars up to 2.5-litre):

1	Marcel Becquart (Jowett)	222.6
2	R.P. Lane (Riley)	227
3	A.P. Warren (Riley)	230.4
4	L.F. Parham (Bristol)	236
5	J.R. Smith (Ford)	239.4
6	R.S. Prout (Austin)	241

Class 3 (Closed cars over 2.5-litre):

1	Percy While (Ford)	240.4
2	J. Park (Allard)	243
3	J.C. Smith (Jaguar)	243.8
4	J.A. Stewart (Bentley)	245.8
5	J.C. Keay (Jaguar)	248.8
6	T.G. Shanley (Austin)	252.2

Ladies' award (Open cars)

Miss M. Newton (Jaguar)

Ladies' award (Closed cars)

Miss C. Sadler (Rover 75)

Team award – SMMT Trophy

Morgans (Peter Morgan, W.A.G. Goodall and Dr W.D. Steel)

Part 3
JWK 651's five brothers

As we have seen in Part 2, JWK 651 had a varied and successful career in three seasons in Leslie Johnson's hands. It was known as 'the car that did everything' – racing, rallying, record-breaking – but was only one of the six special alloy-bodied competition XK 120s that were made in 1950 and that brought Jaguar to prominence in motor sport. The other five cars in this exclusive series were allocated by Jaguar to Nick Haines, Peter Walker, Clemente Biondetti, Ian Appleyard and Tommy Wisdom. The later life of JWK 651 is covered in Part 4 but here we summarise the exploits of those other five cars, together with their owners and drivers.

This painting by Richard Wade specially comissioned by the International Jaguar XK Club depicts the start of the 1950 RAC Tourist Trophy at Dundrod. Leslie Johnson in JWK 651 is already on the move while eventual winner Stirling Moss in Tommy Wisdom's green JWK 988 (660057) is to his left. Peter Whitehead finished second in the red car, which is not one of the six alloy-bodied competition XK 120s but rather the original 1949 car (670002) in which Johnson won the One Hour Production Car Race at Silverstone.
Philip Porter archive

Chapter 11
A winning limited series
The other alloy competition XK 120s

660041

Registration number: MGJ 79
Engine number: W1145-8
Colour: opalescent green
First owner: Nick Haines

This car's first event was the **Mille Miglia on 23 April 1950**. Haines, with co-driver Rudi Haller, ran as high as ninth at Rome but most reports state that they retired after an accident on the return run at Modena, where Haines hit a wall. However, Andrew Whyte, in *Jaguar Sports Racing and Works Competition Cars to 1953*, stated that 'Haines was ninth at Rome but his co-driver Rudi Haller took their car off-course on the drive north, losing too much time to be classified.'

The next outing was **Le Mans on 25 June 1950**. Haines was co-driven on this occasion by Peter Clark and the pair ran as high as eighth until hampered by an oil leak on to the clutch in the closing stages, eventually finishing 12th overall. This was the first-ever Jaguar to make it to the finish at Le Mans.

The only occasion on which this car was rallied was the **Rallye des Alpes, or Alpine Rally, on 2 July 1950**, when Haines was again accompanied by Clark. They experienced brake problems even before they had reached the start at Marseilles, and these continued throughout the event, leading to the car running off the road three times, one involving an 'incident' with a lorry. Haines did manage to get to the finish and take the badly bent car back to the UK for repair.

For the next event, the **One Hour Production Car Race at Silverstone on 26 August 1950**, Tony Rolt was at the wheel of 660041 and finished second in the race for over 2-litre cars behind the XK 120 of Peter Walker. The combined result with the under 2-litre race placed him fourth overall.

During practice for the **Tourist Trophy at Dundrod on 16 September 1950**, Haines crashed the car into a post, but was thankfully only slightly injured. It meant that he and co-driver Tony Rolt were non-starters.

Following the 1950 season, the car was sold by Haines to a family that kept it for three generations until 1986, when it was acquired by long-time Jaguar devotee John Pearson. The car was very complete and original and only required a light restoration, retaining original components such as engine, gearbox, rear axle, body panels and interior trim. The engine was rebuilt by ex-factory man George Hodge, the gearbox and axles by Alan George, and the body by RS Panels. In 2001 the car passed to Charles Bromage and then in spring 2009 it was sold by Fiskens to Dr Hans-Martin Schneeberger, who has owned it for several years and used it on the Mille Miglia and Classic Le Mans events in 2010 and 2012, commenting: 'The car runs great and is a joy to drive.'

Leonard Harry 'Nick' Haines

Of the six original owners of the alloy competition cars, less has been written about Leonard Harry Haines, known as 'Nick', than any other. An Australian, Haines was born in Adelaide in 1911 and grew up in the affluent Sydney harbourside suburb of Rose Bay. He joined the Royal Australian Air Force in the Second World War and was seconded to the RAF, flying distinguished passengers such as Field Marshal Montgomery and Prince Bernhardt of the Netherlands into secret destinations in Europe.

Haines was wealthy and post-war lived at 83 Duke Street, Grosvenor Square, London with his wife Marjorie, whom he had married in 1947. He was the

The first-ever Jaguar to reach the finish line at Le Mans. Nick Haines drove 660041 in the endurance classic in 1950, partnered by Peter Clark. The pair ran as high as eighth until oil leaked on to the clutch, causing them to drop back to 12th at the finish.
Philip Porter archive

A winning limited series

Jaguar XK 120 – JWK 651

A winning limited series

Nick Haines, on the right, with Geoffrey Healey. Haines was Healey's agent in Belgium and later co-founder of the Jaguar distributorship there.
jaguarmagazine.com

proprietor of a prestige car sales business and formed strong associations with both Donald Healey and David Brown of Aston Martin, selling, servicing and supplying spares for both companies, and was also the official distributor for Healey in Belgium.

In 1948 the Healey factory prepared its first two cars for competition, a Saloon (GWD 42) and a Roadster (GWD 43). Both were registered at Warwick on 21 April 1948 in readiness for the Mille Miglia. GWD 42 was the first Healey to leave the starting ramp at Brescia, driven by Haines and Rudi Haller, and it was also the first British car to take part in the event post-war. After passing Rome, and at around 300 miles, a torque rod broke so they found a local garage where it was welded and refitted within 50 minutes, but the car only lasted another 50 miles or so. They continued until the Futa Pass, around two-thirds distance, when the gearbox mainshaft seized and forced them out.

Haines ran the same car in the 1948 Spa 24 Hours with Tommy Wisdom, finishing eighth overall and runner-up in class behind a full-race works Delage. The car also ran at the 12 Hours at Montlhéry but retired because of suspension failure caused by the banked track and poor surface. Later that year Haines achieved a fifth place with the car at Goodwood. His exploits were not confined to the track: he and Donald Healey would have won the 1948 Alpine Trial outright had they not lost 45 minutes helping an injured competitor.

In 1949 Haines became an Aston Martin works driver and ran at Le Mans that year with Arthur Jones in a DB2, but the car was delayed early on the Sunday morning with a troublesome starter motor. Despite a recurrence of the problem, the pair finished seventh overall and third in the 2-litre class. Haines was back at Spa for the 24 Hours again in a DB2, this time with Lance Macklin, finishing fifth.

Haines was a friend of William Lyons and his competition results also left an impression on 'Lofty' England, the head of Jaguar's fledgling XK 120 racing team. It was England who hand-picked the UK-based owners who would receive the six alloy cars to be used for competition.

At around this time Haines became co-founder and owner of the Jaguar distributorship in Belgium. His partner was the forthright and somewhat notorious Madame Joska Bourgeois, who had flown illegally to the UK soon after the war in controversial circumstances. She apparently got herself to Lyons's home and asked him if she could take on Jaguar sales in her home country. Lyons and England were not so sure and only agreed if Haines were to be her equal partner. The Belgian market was such a success for Jaguar that Mark V saloons were even assembled there in the early 1950s after a tax was imposed on imports.

Haines took delivery of 660041 in March 1950 but it spent much of its time in the Experimental Department at Jaguar under Phil Weaver, being prepared to Haines's demanding satisfaction. A large number of modifications were made to all aspects from the engine to carburettors, seats, fuel pump, lights and a speedometer calibrated in kilometres per hour as the car was registered in Belgium.

As described previously, Haines crashed heavily in the first practice session at Dundrod and did not start the Tourist Trophy of 1950. He never raced the car again and was reported to have had enough of tough, high-speed, continental road races. It is likely that the injuries sustained in the crash incapacitated him seriously but he remained a member of the British Racing Drivers' Club until his death, after a long illness, in 1969 in Palma, Majorca, aged just 58.

660042

Registration number: JWK 977
Engine number: W1146-8
Colour: olive green
First owner: Peter Walker

Peter Walker had to miss **Le Mans on 24–25 June 1950** due to commitments on his farm and so 660042 was driven in its maiden race by Peter Whitehead and John Marshall. The pair ran strongly to begin with, lying sixth after two hours, but began to drop back with brake problems, eventually finishing 15th.

At the **One Hour Production Car Race at Silverstone on 26 August 1950** Walker qualified on pole and dominated the whole of the over 2-litre race, coming home ahead of team-mate Tony Rolt. The aggregate result, combined with the under 2-litre race, meant that he finished third overall behind the Ferraris of Alberto Ascari and Dorino Serafini.

Walker took 660042 to two hill climbs, **Prescott on 10 September 1950** and **Shelsley Walsh on 23 September 1950**, winning the over 3-litre sports car class at the latter.

In the **One Hour Production Car Race at Silverstone on 5 May 1951** Walker was lying third until he had to call at his pit with a sticking throttle, eventually finishing 15th, three laps down.

In 1951 the car was sold to Hugh Howorth with C-type parts including rear axle, cylinder head, carburettors and exhaust system. Howorth enjoyed considerable success with the car, including winning the William Lyons Trophy in 1952 and 1954. The car then passed through the hands of six other owners,

Pit stop for the Walker XK120 (660042) at Le Mans 1950, where it was driven by Peter Whitehead and John Marshall. *LAT*

A winning limited series

Peter Walker is seen on the left in this photograph, sitting next to Peter Whitehead, with Duncan Hamilton seated on the right.
Revs Institute for Automotive Research/George Phillips

including David Cottingham, before being purchased by John Foster of Fife. It remained in Foster's ownership for many years, still with its original engine (W1146-8) and is currently in the possession of his son William.

Peter Walker
Known as 'Skid' Walker because of his aggressive driving style, Peter Douglas Conyers Walker was born on 7 October 1912 and began racing Peter Whitehead's ERA in 1935, scoring victories at Brooklands and Donington Park. He finished 11th in the 1948 RAC British Grand Prix at Silverstone, again in an ERA, and the same year set FTD at the Prescott hill climb and came second at one of the first events at the new Goodwood circuit.

A works Jaguar drive in the XK 120's debut race at the International Trophy at Silverstone in 1949 resulted in second place, and the following year, driving 660042, he won the event. Also in 1950 he drove an ERA E-type at the British Grand Prix, but the car failed to finish. Walker took 660042 to Shelsley Walsh later in 1950 and won the over 3-litre class from Sydney Allard.

Le Mans in 1951 brought Walker's greatest success. He had already tested the new Jaguar XK 120C, or C-type, a few weeks before the race, beating the time set by Stirling Moss. He was partnered by Peter Whitehead in a three-car works team along with Stirling Moss/Jack Fairman and Leslie Johnson/Clemente Biondetti. Moss was the early leader of the race and after four hours the three Jaguars held the top three places. After two of the C-types suffered oil pressure problems, it was left to Walker and Whitehead to give Jaguar its first-ever victory at Le Mans.

A month later Walker suffered severe burns racing a BRM V16 at the British Grand Prix, but he still drove a C-type in the Tourist Trophy later that year at Dundrod, finishing runner-up behind Moss in a Jaguar 1-2-3.

For the 1952 Le Mans Walker and Moss were partnered in one of three rebodied, lightweight C-types with long, streamlined nose and elongated tail, but the race was to prove a disaster for the works team. Plumbing changes resulted in overheating and all three cars were out within four hours. The following year was different, though, and once again Walker shared a C-type with Moss. They held an early lead until fuel problems dropped them down the field. With the problem rectified, they charged back to finish second behind team-mates Tony Rolt and Duncan Hamilton.

With 1954 proving an unfruitful year, Walker left Jaguar to join Aston Martin for 1955, winning the Goodwood Nine Hours with Dennis Poore in a DB3S, his only victory of the year. A serious accident in a DB3S at Le Mans in 1956 more or less ended his driving career. Walker took up rabbit and chinchilla farming and died on 1 March 1984.

A winning limited series

660043

Registration number: JWK 650
Engine number: W1147-8
Colour: red
First owner: Jaguar Cars – allocated to Clemente Biondetti

The first of the six alloy competition cars to be completed and the first to run competitively, 660043 was allocated to Clemente Biondetti but ownership was retained by the factory. It was fitted with a speedometer calibrated in kilometres per hour and its first event was the **Targa Florio on 2 April 1950**. Just before half distance Biondetti was lying a remarkable second to Alberto Ascari's Ferrari and ahead of the other works Ferraris when a con-rod broke. The car had been driven out to Italy by John Lea, accompanied by Ron Sutton after Lea had hit a traffic island in Folkestone while avoiding a pedestrian in the rain and had to return for repairs before

Chassis number 660043, raced in 1950 by Clemente Biondetti, sits on the start line at the Mille Miglia. Despite having to stop to repair a broken rear spring, Biondetti finished eighth.

Jaguar XK 120 – JWK 651 | 87

A winning limited series

setting off again. Lea later reported back in a letter to Bill Heynes the events of the Targa:

'Biondetti started off at 5am in the Targa Florio and at 10am his engine failed at Enna when he was lying second behind Ascari in a special 2½-litre Ferrari. This particular car is claimed to weigh 750kg and the engine develops 164bhp. All the (quicker) Ferraris retired for various causes and Biondetti is being cheerfully blamed for pushing them so much that they either burst or went off the road, trying to keep up with the Jaguar. This car caused a sensation over here with its appearance, silence, comfort, tractability and amazing speed. It is gratifying to hear praise from the Italians who have held almost a monopoly of the very fast sports car.'

The car remained in Italy for its second event, the **Mille Miglia on 23 April 1950**, where it was joined by the XK 120s of Haines, Wisdom and Johnson. Biondetti later reported that he had been making good time when he felt the engine begin to misfire, leading to the spark plugs being changed while refuelling. Later a rear spring leaf broke, a consequence of the rough roads and Biondetti's forceful driving. He managed to effect a repair with the help of a local blacksmith who clamped the broken spring and, despite having to keep refilling the radiator, eventually came home eighth.

Biondetti's next event in the car was the **Parma-Poggio di Berceto race on 14 May 1950**, in which he finished third. He dropped out of the **Coppa della Toscana on 4 June 1950** and crashed on the **Giro dell'Umbria on 29 June 1950**, bending the chassis.

The car was eventually returned in bits to the factory in 1953. It was sold to Ron Heegan and then Peter Jacques before being bought by Alec Harvey-Bailey in July 1957.

● Clemente Biondetti has the bonnet up on 660043 during the 1950 Mille Miglia, presumably for one of the many times he had to top up the radiator. *LAT*

Exceptional Cars

Jaguar Driver magazine reported in June 1972 that the car had been bought by London-based Brian Rutland, who intended to restore it to concours standard. In December 1976 Rod Leach's Nostalgia company offered 660043 for sale in *Motor Sport* and four years later, in August 1980, it was advertised in the same magazine by Lynx Engineering: 'XK120 Ex-works Competition lightweight Roadster. Features C-type suspension and other competition mods. Raced by Biondetti in the Mille Miglia and Targa Florio. Concours condition. Registration number JWK 650. £15,000.'

Two years later, in 1982, it was again for sale through DCM, London, in the November issue of *Thoroughbred and Classic Cars*, for £15,450. It is now kept in the Ralph Lauren collection at the Boston Museum of Fine Art.

Clemente Biondetti

Clemente Biondetti was a driver who excelled in Italian endurance events. He won the Mille Miglia four times – more than any other driver – and three of these successes came in consecutive years, 1947–49. He was the first overseas member of the Jaguar team, driving for the works in 1950 and 1951, and he raced his own Jaguar-engined special between 1950 and 1952.

Biondetti was born in Buddusò in Sardinia on 18 August 1898 and started racing motorcycles in 1923 before moving on to cars in 1927. He finished seventh in the 1927 Coppa Ciano, driving a Salmson 1100, and came fourth in the car the following year. In 1928 he finished second in the Tripoli *voiturette* race and then won the event in 1929. In 1930 he came third in a Talbot 700 in the Rome GP and won the Coppa della Consuma in a Bugatti T35. In 1931 Biondetti joined the Maserati factory team, and finished third in both the Rome and the French Grands Prix that year in a Maserati 26M but won the Circuito di Pontedera in a Bugatti T35.

Biondetti's first Mille Miglia was in 1936 driving for Enzo Ferrari's Alfa Romeo team. He broke the record for the run to Bologna but his lead was slowly clawed back by both Giuseppe Farina and Antonio Brivio, also in Alfa Romeos. Brivio won by just 32 seconds, with Biondetti eventually finishing fourth – a fine showing for his first time on the event. In 1937 he was again in an Alfa, an 8C 2900B, but in a race marred by heavy rain he failed to finish. The 1938 Mille Miglia was a different matter. By now Alfa Romeo had absorbed Enzo Ferrari's Scuderia and created a new works team, Alfa Corse, but still run by Ferrari himself, and entered four cars, including a new 8C 2900C for Biondetti. He did not disappoint and led home his team-mate Carlo Pintacuda by two minutes to secure his first major victory.

The same year Biondetti finished second in the *voiturette* class of the Coppa Ciano and third in the main event. He also drove for Alfa in the 24-hour races at Le Mans and Spa in 1938 but did not finish either of them. In 1939 he won the *voiturette* class at the Coppa Acerbo in an Alfa Romeo 158 and came second in the

The spirit of the Mille Miglia – rapt attention from locals as Biondetti's Jaguar blasts through an archway on a cobbled city street.

A winning limited series

Ian and Pat Appleyard won their third consecutive *Coupe des Alpes* for a penalty-free run on the 1952 Alpine Rally in 660044.
Revs Institute for Automotive Research/Rodolfo Mailander

Swiss Grand Prix, just as war intervened.

Following the end of hostilities, the Mille Miglia resumed in 1947 and Biondetti was invited by Emilio Romano to share his 2900 Alfa Romeo *berlinetta* on the event. They chased down the Cisitalia of Tazio Nuvolari and took the lead when he had to stop to change the distributor in torrential rain. The pair won by 16 minutes and the victory gave Alfa Romeo its 11th, and last, triumph in the event.

For the 1948 Mille Miglia, Biondetti was behind the wheel of a coupé-bodied Ferrari 166. His teammate Nuvolari, in a 166 *barchetta*, drove like a man possessed, despite ill-health, and held the lead for much of the event until his brakes failed and he crashed, handing a second successive victory to Biondetti, who had earlier in the year also won the Targa Florio for Ferrari. This double success was repeated in 1949, when Biondetti won the Targa in a Ferrari 166 SC and the Mille Miglia in a 166 MM, leading home team-mate Felice Bonetto.

For 1950 Biondetti was chosen to be one of the six recipients of the alloy competition XK 120s, thereby becoming not only the first overseas Jaguar works driver but also the first person to race an XK 120 on the continent. Alas, his time with Jaguar failed to bring the success he had previously enjoyed.

That same year Biondetti contested his one and only World Championship Formula 1 race, the Italian Grand Prix, driving a self-built Ferrari-Jaguar, but retired for unspecified reasons after 15 laps. He ran this car, which used the rebuilt engine from his Targa Florio XK 120 in a Ferrari chassis, in a number of events around this time and it was described in race results as either a Jaguar Special or a Biondetti Special.

In 1951 he drove a works C-type at Le Mans, sharing with Leslie Johnson, but the pair had to retire with oil pump failure while lying third. In 1952 he finished third in the Monaco Grand Prix, run for sports cars that year, driving a Ferrari 225 S. Other good results that year were third place at Vila Real in a Ferrari 166 MM, second in the 12 Hours of Pescara in a 225 S, and victory in the 10 Hours of Messina in a Ferrari 212 Export.

The 1953 season brought a single victory, in the Coppa della Toscana driving a Lancia Aurelia, while he took a Lancia D20 to eighth place in the Mille Miglia.

In his last season, 1954, he won the Bari three-hour race in a Ferrari 375 Mondial and finished fourth at the Reims 12 Hours co-driving a 375 MM with Masten Gregory. In Ferrari 250 MM models he was fourth in the Mille Miglia and the Monza 1,000Km, and fifth in the Targa Florio.

At the end of the season Biondetti was forced to retire from racing, having been suffering for some time from cancer. He died on 24 February 1955 in Florence.

660044

Registration number: NUB 120
Engine number: W1148-8
Colour: white
First owner: Ian Appleyard

This car, a particularly famous XK 120, was allocated to Ian Appleyard for rallying. It was campaigned by him with his wife Pat, the daughter of William Lyons, acting as navigator. Appleyard wrote of his impression of the XK 120: 'In common with every motoring enthusiast in the country, my ambition became to drive that Jaguar. It seemed to exemplify everything that was desirable in a car…'

The couple's first event was the **Tulip Rally on 16–22 April 1950** where they were set for victory until incurring a penalty for not quite crossing a white line during a driving test. Appleyard was so annoyed with himself that he entered the **Morecambe Rally** in order gain more experience in these special tests and came away with the Lancashire Cup for best performance by a

Braking test on the 1953 RAC Rally of Great Britain, which the Appleyards won in NUB 120. The car was uprated to Special Equipment spec for the 1953 season.
The Revs Institute for Automotive Research/George Phillips

Exceptional Cars

A winning limited series

Jaguar XK 120 – JWK 651

A winning limited series

'Appleyard is best remembered for his rally exploits in NUB 120, his gleaming white XK120'

production car.

All this was by means of preparation for their next event, the **Alpine Rally on 13 July 1950**. Extra equipment fitted for the Alpine included two large-dial aircraft-type stop-clocks mounted on the dashboard and illuminated with a special light for the first night's run in the dark. Close to these was an extra horn button connected to a Klaxon mounted low down at the front of the car. The car had a 24-gallon fuel tank, carried two spare wheels, cans of oil, a spare inner tube, and replacement water hoses and light bulbs. The preparation and attention to detail paid off and the Appleyards completed the event without a single penalty point, winning a *Coupe des Alpes*.

Back home, in September they won a first-class award on the **Lakeland Rally** and the **East Anglian MC's rally to Clacton**. Two months later, in November, they finished second in the Motor Cycling Club's **1,000-Mile Rally**.

The 1951 season began with the **Tulip Rally** in April, and this time there were no mistakes, the Appleyards taking victory. Another win followed in the **Morecambe Rally** and at the revived **RAC Rally**, the first since 1939. But the big one was the **Alpine Rally** and the couple repeated their success of the previous year, winning another *Coupe des Alpes*. Journalist Gordon Wilkins navigated for Appleyard on the **London Rally**, which they won, while Pat took over the driving of NUB 120 on the **Lakeland Rally** with Ian as navigator, winning the ladies' prize.

In 1952 the Appleyards finished third on the **RAC Rally** while for the **Morecambe Rally** the car was lent to a friend of theirs, E. Ainsworth, who drove it without any success. Once again, it was the **Alpine Rally** that really mattered and for this NUB 120 was fitted with centre-lock wire wheels and self-adjusting front brakes. The Appleyards realised that an outright win was now unlikely with a car of NUB 120's age and so concentrated on ensuring that they did not concede any penalty points. This they achieved for the third consecutive year, thus earning a Gold Cup for the car, which became in great demand for displays and other publicity purposes.

By 1953, NUB 120 was being used less frequently, but Appleyard brought it out for a third **RAC Rally**, the car having been uprated to 'Special Equipment spec', and took victory. The final competitive fling for NUB 120 was the **1953 Morecambe Rally**, which it again won.

By now NUB 120 had covered around 50,000 competitive miles and was bought back by Jaguar from Appleyard, who replaced it with a new XK 120, registration number RUB 120. The original spent a long time on display at the National Motor Museum at Beaulieu and is now kept at the Jaguar Heritage Trust, maintained in full working order but still in original condition, and shown at classic car events.

Ian Appleyard

Described in his obituary in *The Independent* as a 'sporting icon for his generation', Ernest Ian Appleyard was born 10 October 1923 in Linton, West Yorkshire. He obtained a degree in mechanical engineering in 1943 and went on to become a Major at the Royal Military Academy of Science. He played tennis for Yorkshire and skied for Britain in the 1948 Winter Olympic Games, finishing 55th in the men's slalom and 91st in the men's downhill. However, it is for his exploits as a rally driver, in his gleaming white Jaguar XK 120, NUB 120, that he is best remembered.

Appleyard's connections with Jaguar were strong. His father ran the Jaguar dealership, Appleyard of Leeds, of which he became a director in 1946, and he married Patricia, the elder daughter of William and Greta Lyons.

Ian Appleyard, together with his wife Pat – daughter of William Lyons – as navigator, enjoyed considerable success with 660044. *LAT*

Appleyard really made his name by competing in the Alpine Rally. In 1947 he finished third in class driving a Jaguar SS 100 (EXT 207), while the following year he received factory support in another SS 100 (LNW 100) and won his first *Coupe des Alpes* (Alpine Cup), achieving all the target times despite stopping to help a rival competitor.

He drove with Donald Healey in a Healey Silverstone (JAC 100) in the 1949 event, the pair finishing second overall and winning their class. For 1950 he was back in a Jaguar, NUB 120, which he drove with his wife Pat. This was the start of something very special because between 1950 and 1952 the pair finished the Alpine Rally three times in the same car without incurring any penalties. Appleyard thus became the first driver to win the *Coupe d'Or* (Gold Cup). Only two other drivers would go on to equal this achievement, Stirling Moss in 1954 and Jean Vinatier in 1971.

A fifth *Coupe des Alpes* followed in 1953, but Appleyard had also achieved successes elsewhere – he won the Tulip Rally in 1951 and the RAC Rally in 1951 and 1953, finishing runner-up on the Monte Carlo Rally the same year in a Jaguar Mark VII. His last notable result was second on the 1956 RAC Rally in an XK 140.

After retiring from rallying, he was chairman of the Appleyard Group until 1988 and returned to his childhood love of ornithology, becoming a leading authority on the subject of the Ring Ouzel. Appleyard died in Harrogate, North Yorkshire, on 2 June 1998.

A winning limited series

It was with a young Stirling Moss behind the wheel that Tommy Wisdom's 660057 enjoyed its greatest triumph, winning the 1950 RAC Tourist Trophy at Dundrod in torrential rain and gale-force winds. *LAT*

660057

Registration number: JWK 988
Engine number: W1311-8
Colour: apple green
First owner: Tommy Wisdom and Bill Cannell

This right-hand-drive car was allocated to 43-year-old Tommy Wisdom, the motoring editor of the *Daily Herald*, *The People* and *Sporting Life*.

Wisdom's first outing in 660057 was the **Mille Miglia on 23 April 1950**, co-driven by Anthony Hume, the pair retiring only 30 miles from the finish when the gearbox jammed owing to a misplaced synchro ring, the car having already been delayed by a loose wheel and a sticking throttle.

The next event was the **Circuito do Porto on 18 June**. The car was driven to Portugal by service engineer Ken Bowen, who reported:

'The car ran beautifully on the 1,485 mile journey to Oporto. Absolutely no trouble of any kind was experienced. The race commenced with Mr Wisdom on the front row, having secured second fastest practice time. Getting away to a grand start, Mr Wisdom occupied second place to Bonetto's 4½ litre Alfa Romeo until late in the race. He finished third, having been passed by Carini's OSCA.'

Fading brakes had caused Wisdom to slow during the final six laps of the race, after which Bowen drove the car to Le Mans for the following weekend's 24-hour race. Wisdom had agreed that his car could be used for spares for the three XK 120s that were competing there, as he was driving a Jowett Jupiter with Tommy Wise, the pair finishing 16th and winning their class.

In August the car was entered for the **One Hour Production Car Race at Silverstone on 26 August** but Wisdom was well off the pace in the event, finishing seventh. However, he saw Stirling Moss win the supporting 500cc event and finish sixth in the Formula 1 race and later agreed to let him drive 660057 in the **Tourist Trophy at Dundrod on 16 September**.

Moss had been refused a drive at Dundrod by the works Jaguar team on the grounds of his youth and inexperience, but his performance there proved the doubters wrong. In atrocious conditions he set the fastest time in practice and simply drove away from the rest of the field to earn his first international win.

Wisdom raced the car only twice in 1951, at the **One Hour Production Car Race at Silverstone on 5 May**, where he finished ninth, and again at the Circuito do Porto for the **Portuguese Grand Prix on 17 June**, retiring this time.

The car was sold by the end of 1951. In the early 1960s it was owned by Malcolm Elder who used it as a road car but also raced it at Silverstone a couple of times. In the mid-1960s it was owned by Peter Butt, in the 1970s by David Cottingham and then, briefly by Bob Smith of RS Panels, before returning to

A winning limited series

Tommy Wisdom, right, with Leslie Johnson, with whom he shared a Nash-Healey at Le Mans in 1952.
Revs Institute for Automotive Research/George Phillips

Cottingham, who set about having it restored, a task that was completed in 1984. It is now owned by JCB chairman Lord Bamford.

Tommy Wisdom

A motoring journalist and gentleman racer, Thomas Henry Wisdom was born in Brighton on 16 February 1906. His wife Elsie, affectionately known as 'Bill', was also an accomplished driver and the pair were invited by William Lyons to take one of the new SS 100 models on the 1936 Alpine Trial, which they won. The following year he won at Brooklands with a specially lightened and tuned SS 100. Among the many other makes of cars he drove were Aston Martin, Bristol, Healey, Jowett, Riley, Singer and Talbot.

Through the 1930s Wisdom competed in events such as the RAC Tourist Trophy and the 500 Miles of Brooklands. His first Le Mans was in 1934, driving a Singer Le Mans with John Donald Barnes, the pair finishing 18th. Although a full-time journalist, Wisdom was a prolific competitor and took part in the Monte Carlo Rally 23 times, the Le Mans 24 Hours 11 times, the Mille Miglia 10 times and the Targa Florio four times; he won his class in the Mille Miglia in 1949 and 1952 and at Le Mans in 1950 and 1952.

In 1949 Wisdom was one of the invited journalists who went to Jabbeke in Belgium to witness the first public speed demonstration of the new XK 120. He and Walter Hassan, Jaguar's development engineer, took the prototype on a recce for the Alpine Rally, which was dominated the following year for Jaguar by Ian Appleyard. In 1949 he also finished sixth at Le Mans in a Bentley 4¼ Paulin with Jack 'Zoltan' Hay.

Wisdom was one of the chosen six to receive an alloy XK 120 for 1950, as explained on the previous page, and he raced it into 1951.

For the 1951 Mille Miglia, however, Wisdom forsook the XK 120 for an Aston Martin DB2, and finished 11th with Anthony Hume. At Le Mans he was once more in a Jowett Jupiter with Wise but the pair retired.

In the 1952 Mille Miglia Wisdom again drove an Aston Martin, this time with Fred Lown, achieving a class victory and 12th place overall. Wisdom and Cannell had ordered a C-type Jaguar (XKC 005) when it was announced and Wisdom drove it in the 1952 Monaco Grand Prix, run for sports cars that year, finishing sixth. He also recorded his best finish at Le Mans in 1952 driving a Nash-Healey with Leslie Johnson to third place.

The 1953 season brought less success, Wisdom retiring an Aston Martin DB2 from the Mille Miglia and a Bristol 450 at Le Mans. In 1954 he and Jack Fairman took a Bristol 450 to eighth place at Le Mans and 12th place in the 12 Hours of Reims. His last Le Mans start was in 1955, again in a Bristol 450 with Fairman, the pair finishing ninth.

In 1959 Wisdom was part of the three-driver BMC team that set 12 speed records at Bonneville Salt Flats with the EX-219 experimental Austin-Healey Sprite.

He died in Birmingham on 12 November 1972.

Part 4
Later life of JWK 651

After such a hectic life under the ownership of Leslie Johnson, it was perhaps time for JWK 651 to enjoy a well-earned rest and a bit of TLC. Its next owner was Leslie Lefever, who used the car as personal transport for a number of years, before it passed through a succession of owners who, in turn, stamped their own personality on the car, even changing the engine and having louvres cut into the body. Happily, most of the original parts, including the engine, were eventually reunited with the car and gradually, over time and piece by piece, it has been lovingly restored to its original 1950 Le Mans specification.

● JWK 651 looks magnificent as drivers Derek Cooper and Olaf Meyer eagerly anticipate the start of the 2011 Mille Miglia. *JD Classics*

Chapter 12
Over the years
Road use and back to racing

Leslie Johnson sold JWK 651 to Leslie Charles Lefever of Woodford Green, Essex in 1952, although Lefever's widow Audrey thinks that the purchase may have been transacted through her father-in-law's company. This was around the time that Lefever, who was something of a motor sport enthusiast, accompanied Leslie Johnson on the 1952 RAC Rally – and as rally documentation notes that Johnson was number two driver to Lefever, perhaps the transaction had been completed shortly before the event.

Audrey Lefever told how shortly after the rally she and her husband went on their honeymoon with JWK 651, although soon the car was sent back to Jaguar where, she said, it was fitted with standard bench seating finished in two-tone pigskin with red piping. And, claimed Mrs Lefever, they also came away with a spare hide to cover their dining room chairs!

Thereafter the Lefevers used the car as family transport, reputedly even towing a caravan with it, until, early in the 1960s, the family business ran into financial trouble. According to Mrs Lefever, JWK 651 was then probably taken by the receivers, R.P. Ellen, and she thought it was they who applied for the duplicate logbook so that it could be sold. In June 1964 it was bought by Anthony Michael Foley of 12 Pindock Mews, Little Venice, London W9. Foley's name appears after Lefever's unsigned entry in the duplicate buff logbook that accompanies the car today.

In October 1965 this logbook records the registered keeper as changing to Donald Wilson of Millbrook, Southampton, but within a year or two JWK 651 was back in Pindock Mews where it was being retailed once more by Foley, this time in partnership with Peter Butt. Noted Jaguar author Paul Skilleter paints this picture of the London XK scene during this period:

'Pindock Mews was something of a mecca for XK enthusiasts at this time, mainly because Peter Butt specialised in preparing and selling XKs, mostly XK 120 roadsters and mostly to impecunious youngsters like me. They were just regarded as old sports cars – the term "classic car" did not exist.

'Prices typically averaged around the £125 mark, but besides all the run-of-the-mill steel roadsters, Peter would quite often acquire (and indeed rescue) more significant XKs and a number of aluminium and ex-works XK 120s passed through his hands in the 1960s and early 1970s. These, even by the prices of the day, were beyond my slender resources but in 1968 I did manage to buy LXK 48 (670144) from Peter. In the spring of 1971 he organised a cosmetic refurbishment for me which included painting LXK cream as I was going motor racing and wanted it to look like Leslie Johnson's car – which I had seen in the Mews around the time I bought LXK two or three years earlier.

'By the time I first encountered JWK 651 around 1968, it had already acquired its non-period "extras", because, Peter told me, it had looked far too ordinary on its pressed steel wheels and standard bodywork, and to shift an XK for more than £400 in those days meant wire wheels at the very least... As he was breaking an XK 150 at the time, Peter removed 651's original engine and slotted in the 150's 3.4 unit, along with the later car's front suspension and rear axle complete. These conveniently provided both disc

JWK 651 on the road in 1999 driven by then owner Hugh Palmer and photographed for an article in *Jaguar World* magazine.
Paul Skilleter photo archive

Over the years

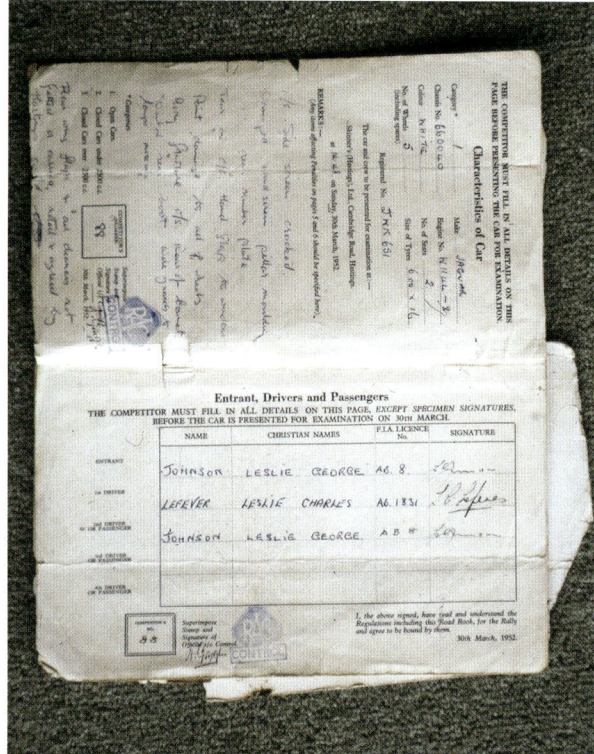

● The completed entry form for the 1952 RAC Rally, during which Leslie Johnson was accompanied by future owner Leslie Lefever.

Wire wheels, bonnet and ● wing louvres – and a 3.8-litre engine – were fitted to JWK 651 in the 1960s and the modifications remained when Michael Rowan acquired it 1976.
Paul Skilleter photo archive

brakes and the mandatory wire wheels. The bench seating was replaced by sportier bucket seats, and as the instrument panel looked boringly standard Peter fitted a big old Lagonda rev counter he had lying around. Finally, he arranged for a local body shop to fit louvres not only in the bonnet but also in the front and rear wings... But with considerable foresight, Peter kept all the parts he removed, to the great benefit of the car and its later owners'.

It is a little difficult to pin down exactly when these modifications, which the car retained for decades, were actually made. A letter exists written by Foley to a potential buyer, John Stringer of Dorchester, who was interested in purchasing JWK 651; this letter describes the car as having a 3.8-litre engine, wire wheels and Koni shock absorbers. The letter is undated but John Stringer, in 1997, put the year at 1966. However, the changes may possibly have been made a little later, as JWK 651 did not leave Pindock Mews for a new owner until June 1969, when it was sold to John Panton of Wokingham, Berkshire.

Panton was famous among XK enthusiasts for owning no fewer than three very rare right-hand-drive XK 140 roadsters. He and JWK 651 were regularly to be seen at Jaguar Drivers' Club XK Register events until Michael Rowan acquired the car in 1976. It then remained unseen for many years and was thought to have been shipped abroad until it was learned in 1990 that the car was still in Rowan's London garage.

JWK 651 was offered for sale at the Coys 'True Greats' auction at the Royal Horticultural Halls, London, on 14 December 1995 with an estimate of £80,000–£100,000 but failed to sell.

For many years the whereabouts of JWK 651 were unknown until it resurfaced in Michael Rowan's garage in 1990.
JD Classics

Over the years

Auction description
Coys 'True Greats' Auction, The Royal Horticultural Halls, London, 14 December 1995
Lot 033: Jaguar XK120 Competition (1950)
Lot Number 033
Estimate £80,000-£100,000
Year 1950
Condition rating 3
Registration number JWK 651
Chassis number 660040
Engine number W11448

Although the engine number quoted by Coys is that of the original, this is not correct and it is thought that the details had been read from the chassis plate without checking the number of the engine installed.

The car was then purchased by Hugh Palmer via Classic Automobiles in 1997. Palmer managed to acquire the original engine, W1144-8, together with the original seats, frames and runners, suspension units, steering wheel, road wheels and quick-filler fuel cap from Peter Butt in February 1999. This is confirmed in a letter from Butt to Palmer in which he refers to 'all items removed by myself from the Leslie

● Hugh Palmer, who purchased JWK 651 in 1997, is pictured with the original seats and engine which, together with many other parts, he was later able to acquire from Peter Butt.
Paul Skilleter photo archive

Exceptional Cars

Hugh Palmer proudly displays Audrey Lefever's Mille Miglia silk scarf, a souvenir of the 1951 event in which Leslie Johnson crashed JWK 651 after hitting a patch of oil. *Paul Skilleter photo archive*

Johnson works Jaguar JWK 651 in the mid 1960s'.

Palmer had the engine refitted and had some remedial work carried out on the car, mostly to strengthen the ash framing, which had deteriorated in some places. A major article on the car by Paul Skilleter appeared in the Vol 11 no 5 June 1999 issue of *Jaguar World* magazine.

Palmer then entered JWK 651 in the Coys Historic Festival auction at Rockingham on 27 May 2001. London solicitor and car collector Peter Mimpriss bought the car for £222,700 – thought to be a record price for any XK 120 sold up until that time.

'Peter Mimpriss bought the car for £222,700 – thought to be a record price for any XK 120 sold up until that time'

Over the years

- Following a brief spell of ownership by Peter Mimpriss, JWK 651 was advertised for sale by Gregor Fisken in 2004 and purchased by Paul Michaels of Hexagon.
Philip Porter archive

Auction description
Coys Historic Festival, Rockingham
The Jaguar Marque, Sports Racing, GT and Touring Cars, Coys, Corby sales centre, 27th May 2001
Lot 181: Jaguar XK120 Aluminium (1950)
Year 1950
Condition rating 2
Registration number JWK 651
Chassis number 660040
Hammer Price (inc premium) £222,700

Mimpriss explained: 'What I like is really interesting, original cars and this seemed to be as original as I was likely to get for a car which had raced and rallied so extensively. This was adding to an existing collection but I didn't have a Jaguar and I thought it would be an interesting car to have.'

Unfortunately Mimpriss immediately identified a drawback with his purchase. 'I went to collect it and drove it back. I then found it was acutely uncomfortable,' he said. 'It was for my personal use

but there wasn't enough room. I like a car where I can stretch my legs out and it was cramped. I used it to a certain extent but I did find it uncomfortable and it was also extremely unreliable. I was quite busy at the time and I found it a bit irritating. If I'd thought about it and had more time I could have had the engine sorted and things like that, in which case it would have had reliability, but even so I still wouldn't have wanted to go on a long journey because I didn't find it at all comfortable.

'I didn't have any restoration work done. If I buy an original car I want it unrestored as far as possible, so I wanted to keep it like that, but I should have taken it to somebody who could have got it working OK without restoring it. I didn't keep it for very long and then I decided to sell it and buy something else.'

The car was advertised for sale by Gregor Fisken and was purchased by Paul Michaels of Hexagon in 2004.

'I was at the Monaco Classic Car Grand Prix, staying with a friend,' explained Michaels. 'He had a copy of

While owned by Paul Michaels, JWK 651 took part in the 'Tribute to Stirling Moss' parade at the Goodwood Revival in 2009, driven by John Coombs.
Chas Parker

Jaguar XK 120 – JWK 651 | 105

Over the years

● Driving JWK 651, Derek Hood of JD Classics leads a C-type and D-type in the 2010 Le Mans Classic.
JD Classics

Jarrah Venables rounds La Source hairpin at Spa in JWK 651, which he shared with Wil Arif, during the RAC Woodcote Trophy race at the 2010 Spa Six Hours meeting, the pair finishing in fifth place. ●
JD Classics

a magazine which I picked up, saw the car advertised and thought, I fancy that. And I bought it on the phone, from Gregor, while I was in Monaco.'

Once he had purchased it, Michaels undertook a complete restoration of the car.

'It had gone through a period when nothing had been spent on it,' he explained. 'There was only one choice – you either left it as it was or you did it properly. It all got done and the car was then lovely.'

While it was in Michaels' ownership, JWK 651 took

Over the years

part in the Fordwater Trophy at the 2008 Goodwood Revival, driven by Stephen Bond. 'I picked a driver who didn't want to make a name for himself because obviously I was petrified that the thing wouldn't come back in one piece.' Bond did bring the car home in one piece, finishing in 10th place.

JWK 651 was back at the Goodwood Revival a year later with John Coombs at the wheel, but this time as part of a 'Tribute to Stirling Moss' parade on the occasion of his 80th birthday, when 80 of the cars in which he competed were assembled on the grid and paraded around the circuit on each of the three days of the event.

Shortly after this, Michaels put the car up for sale and on 6 March 2010 it was purchased by Derek Hood of JD Classics. Since then, the car has once again undergone a complete restoration, returning it to the exact works specification when it ran at Le Mans in 1950. At the time of purchase, the car was still on wire wheels but it has now been returned to pressed steel wheels and drum brakes, and the louvres in the front and rear wings removed, all in a gradual process, the louvres having disappeared by the end of 2011.

Hood has competed in the car a number of times at prestigious historic meetings. Most recently he was 16th overall and the highest-placed XK 120 in Plateau Two at the 2014 Le Mans Classic and finished ninth in the Fordwater Trophy at the 2015 Goodwood Revival.

● Former Jaguar European Touring Car driver Chuck Nicholson was behind the wheel of JWK 651 at the 2011 Goodwood Festival of Speed.
JD Classics

Exceptional Cars

Over the years

For a while the car was owned by a US collector. He had it displayed at Pebble Beach in California before selling it back to JD Classics, which looks after and campaigns the car on behalf of its current owner.

Derek Hood thinks that JWK 651 is a very special car but then, as its custodian, perhaps he is biased. Previous owner Paul Michaels referred to it as 'my favourite white Jaguar'. What is clear is that the car has been very special in its own way to each of its owners, from Leslie Johnson onwards. From a historical viewpoint, it is the most important Jaguar XK of all. To have taken part at Le Mans, the Mille Miglia, the RAC Rally, and record-breaking with Stirling Moss, is 'exceptional' indeed.

Familiar surroundings. Having taken part in the Mille Miglia in 1950 and 1951, JWK 651 was back in 2011 driven by Derek Cooper and Olaf Meyer.
JD Classics

Modern race history

Year	Date	Location	Event	No.	Driver(s)	Result
2008	19–21 September	Goodwood	Fordwater Trophy	23	Stephen Bond	10th
2009	18–20 September	Goodwood	Tribute to Stirling Moss Parade	–	John Coombs	–
2010	9–11 July	Le Mans, France	Le Mans Classic	54	Derek Hood	15th (Race 1)
	24–26 September	Spa-Francorchamps, Belgium	RAC Woodcote Trophy	54	Wil Arif and Jarrah Venables	5th
2011	1–3 July	Goodwood	Festival of Speed	–	Chuck Nicholson	–
	11–15 May	Brescia, Italy	Mille Miglia	–	Derek Cooper and Olaf Meyer	Finisher
2012	16–20 May	Brescia, Italy	Mille Miglia	–	Mike Tuke and Simon Tuke	Finisher
2013	18 August	Pebble Beach Concours d'Elegance	Phil Hill Trophy winner	–	–	2nd in Class 0-1: Post-war Sports and Custom Coachwork
2014	4–6 July	Le Mans, France	Le Mans Classic	70	Derek Hood	16th overall (Plateau 2)
2015	11–13 September	Goodwood Revival	Fordwater Trophy	16	Derek Hood	9th

Over the years

● In the 2014 Le Mans Classic, Derek Hood of JD Classics took JWK 651 to 16th overall, and highest-placed Jaguar XK 120, in Plateau 2.
JD Classics

At the 2015 Goodwood Revival, ●
Derek Hood of JD Classics
drove JWK 651 to ninth place
in the Fordwater Trophy.
JD Classics

Chapter 13
Photo gallery

An exceptional car is now back in exceptional condition. It has had an eventful life: been raced, rallied, made record runs, taken to the shops and been altered and restored by various owners, but today JWK 651 is just as it was when raced at Le Mans in 1950 by Leslie Johnson and Bert Hadley. Every care has been taken to ensure that its specification is exact, every detail accurate, which is nothing less, of course, than a car of this heritage deserves. It is quite simply stunning, as this gallery of superb photographs by John Colley shows.

● Restored to its former glory and carrying its race number '17', just as it did on that bright and sunny afternoon in June 1950 when it lined up to make its competition debut in Les Vingt-Quatre Heures du Mans.

● Immaculate in its Old English White livery, chassis number 660040, better known by its registration JWK 651, is fully equipped with the same spotlights and small aero screen that it had at Le Mans. Overleaf, the rear view shows the quick-action filler cap feeding the 25-gallon fuel tank.

● A plaque on the dashboard records the illustrious history of JWK 651 while above the instruments sits the rear-view mirror and aero screen.

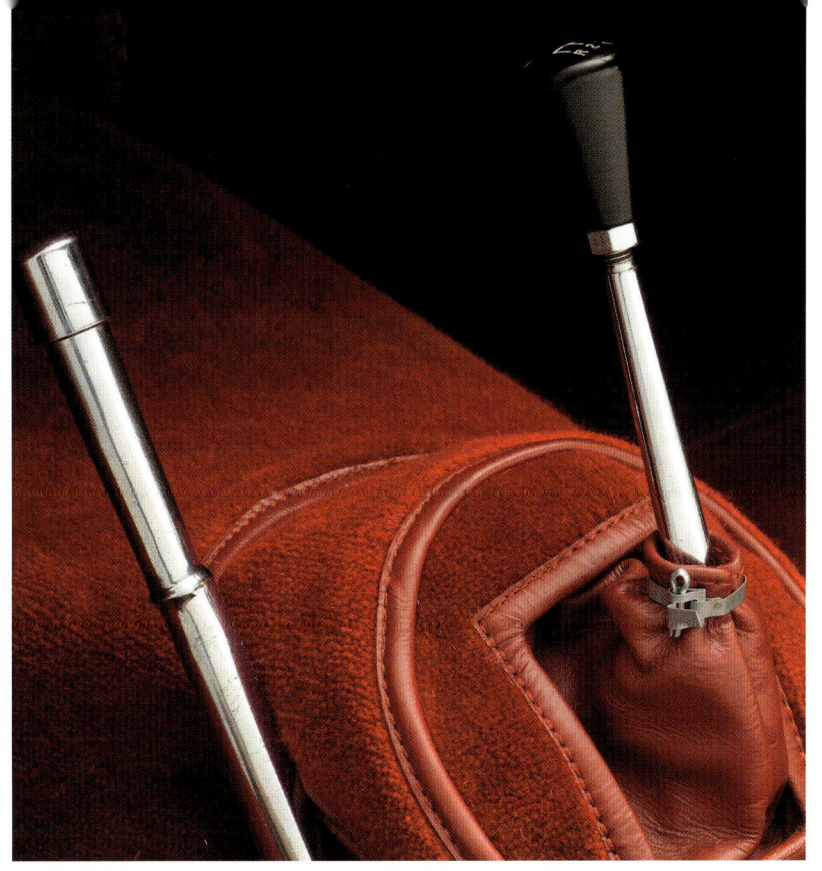

Trimmed in red leather, JWK 651 carries the names of owner Leslie Johnson and Bert Hadley, his co-driver at Le Mans in 1950. The well-worn bonnet strap sits above the iconic Jaguar badge.

- With the bonnet open, JWK 651 reveals its original 3,442cc, six-cylinder XK engine. This engine, number W1144-8, was reunited with the car during its ownership by Hugh Palmer.

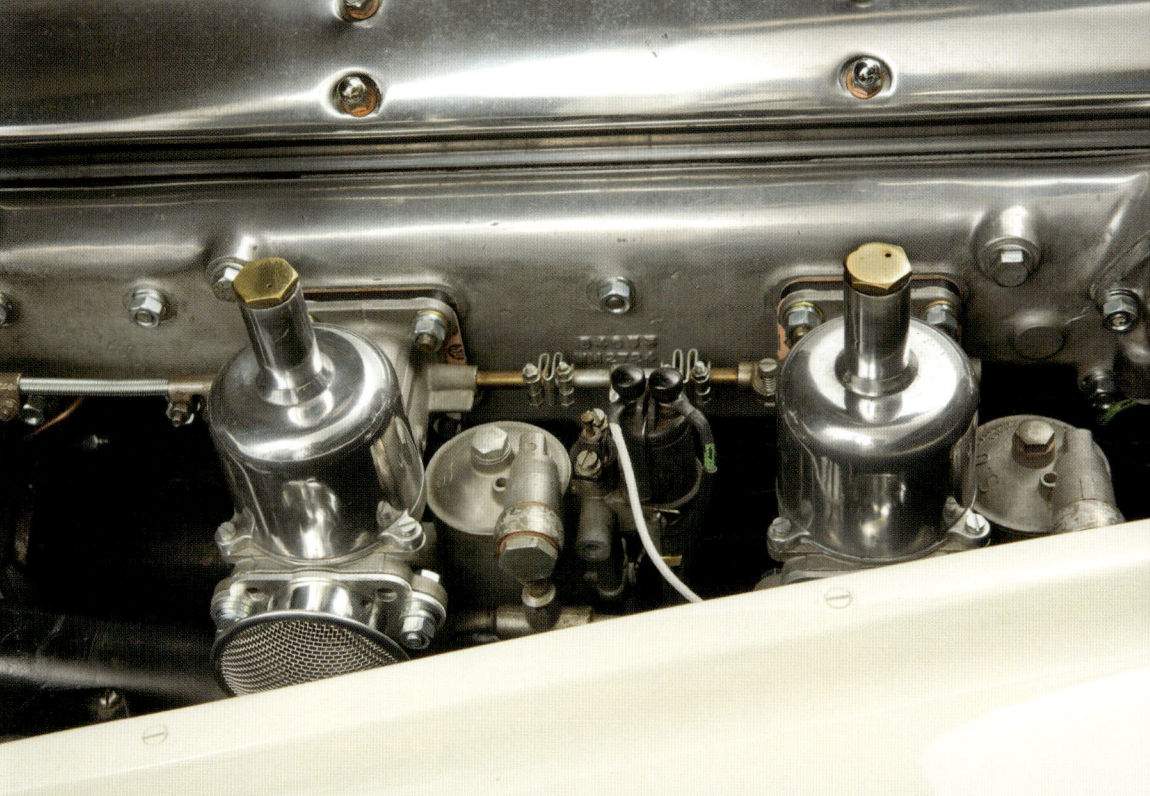

Original chassis plate confirms this is 660040, fitted with body number F1182, engine W1144-8 and gearbox JH2244. Tall 'chimney pot' SU H6 carburettors are as fitted when raced at Le Mans.

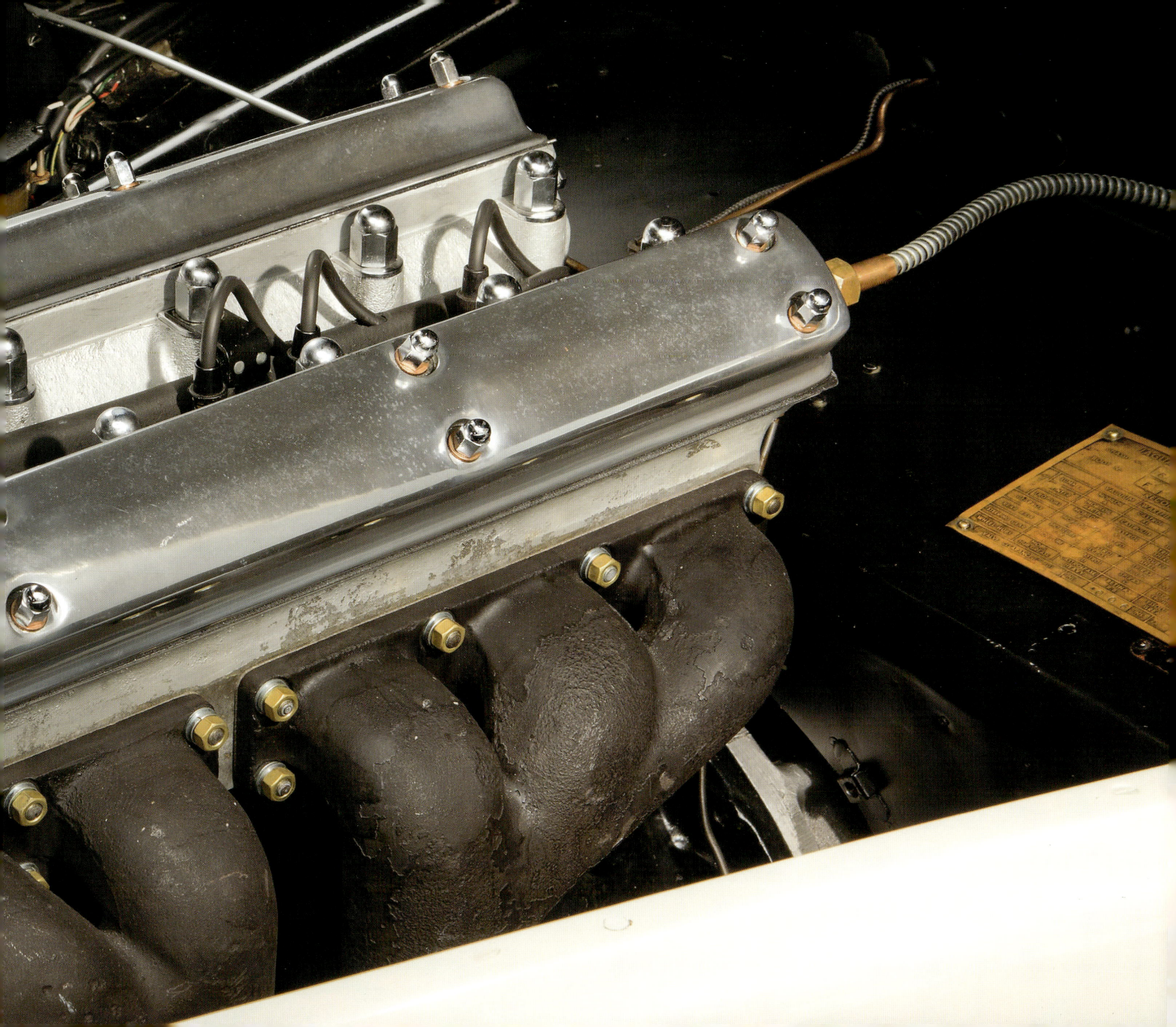

● Celebrated number plate, standard Lucas rear light, and filler pipe leading to 25-gallon fuel tank.

Restored to its former ● glory, JWK 651 sits on its pressed steel wheels awaiting the start of the next chapter of its life.

Acknowledgements

Thanks must be given to all those who gave willingly of their time in order to assist with the research for this book. In particular: Paul Skilleter, James Fraser, Derek Hood, Dr Hugh Palmer, Peter Mimpriss, Paul Michaels, John Pearson, Chris Keith-Lucas, Dr Hans-Martin Schneeberger and Ed Foster.

Apologies to those whose names we have omitted to mention. You know who you are and you have our eternal gratitude.

Index

Abecassis, George 43, 56
Ainsworth, E 92
Alfa Romeo 6C 36, 70
    8C 89
    412 36, 70
Allard J2 43, 52, 56, 70, 74
Allard, Sydney 43, 56, 70
Appleyard, Ian & Pat 20, 74, 78, 79, 80, 90-93
Arif, Will 107
Ascari, Alberto 36, 52, 70, 85
Aston Martin DB1 34
    DB2 34, 43, 52, 56, 70, 84, 95
    DB3S 86
Baily, Claude 12
Bamford, Lord 95
Behra, Jean 43
Berry, Bob 39
Biondetti, Clemente 18, 20, 34, 36, 38, 70, 80, 86, 87-90
Bira, Prince 13, 16
Bond, Stephen 108
Bonetto, Felice 70, 90, 94
Bornigia, Mario & Franco 70
Bourgeois, Joska 84
Bowen, Ken 94
Bracco, Giovanni 39, 70
Brackenbury, Charles 34, 43
Bristol 450, 95
BRM V16 34, 86
Broadhead, Jack 76, 79
Bromage, Charles 82
Butt, Peter 94, 98, 102
Cadillac Coupe de Ville/'Le Monstre' 43, 46
Casse, Michel 43
Chinetti, Luigi 40, 43
Christie, Tom 76

Clark, Peter 18, 20, 40, 82
Cole, Tom 43
Collier, Sam & Miles 43
Coombs, John 105, 108
Cooper-Climax T43 68
Cooper, Derek 97, 109
Cortese, Franco 70
Cottingham, David 86, 94
Crook, Tony 56
Culpan, Norman 14, 56
Cunningham, Briggs 43
De Graffenreid, Baron 66
Dodson, Charlie 66
Elder, Malcolm 94
England, 'Lofty' 13, 16, 18, 40, 56
ERA 34, 39, 86
Fairman, Jack 18, 35, 66, 86, 95
Fangio, Juan Manuel 36, 43, 69
Ferrari 166 36, 40, 52, 70, 90
    195S 36, 40
    275S 36
    340 70
Fisken, Gregor 82, 105
'Flack, T' 58, 61
Foley, Anthony 98, 101
Foster, John 86
Frazer Nash 56, 70
Gable, Clark 15
Gardner, Lt Col. 'Goldie' 12
Gerard, Bob 56
Gonzales, Frolian 43
Gordini, Aldo 43
Gordon, John 43
Gregory, Ken 68
Hadley, Bert 18, 35, 40, 46, 51, 112

Haines, Nick 18, 20, 36, 40, 52, 56, 80, 82-84
Haller, Rudi 82, 84
Hamilton, Duncan 43, 52, 86
Harvey-Bailey, Alec 88
Hassan, Walter 12, 13, 18, 20, 95
Healey, Donald 38, 70, 84
    Geoffrey 38, 70, 84
Healey Silverstone 52, 58, 92
Heegan, Ron 88
'Helde' 43
Heynes, Bill 12, 18, 20, 22, 34, 40
Hood, Derek 106, 108, 109, 110, 111
Horsfall, St John 'Jock' 32, 34
Howorth, Hugh 85
Hume, Anthony 94, 95
Imhof, Godfrey 74, 79
Jaguar C-type 18, 19, 34, 35, 39, 66, 68
Jaguar D-type 69
Jaguar Mark VII 68, 69
Jaguar SS100 92, 95
Jaguar XK120
    Drop Head Coupe 17, 19
    Fixed Head Coupe 16, 19, 66
    HKV 500 13, 14, 34, 72, 80
    Open Two-Seater Super Sports 17, 19
    Special Equipment 19, 91
Jacques, Peter 88
Jenkinson, Denis 69
Johnson, Leslie 13, 14, 18, 20, 31, 32-33, 36, 40, 52, 56,
    62, 66, 70, 74, 86, 95, 97, 98, 112
Jones, Arthur 84
Jowett Jupiter 56, 94, 95
Lancia Aurelia 70, 73, 90
Lauren, Ralph 89
Lea, John 36, 38, 70, 87
Leach, Rod 89
Lefever, Leslie 97, 98, 100
Leygonie, Pierre 43
Lotus 18 69
Loyer, Roger 43
Lucas, Jean 43
Lyons, Sir William 18, 84, 93, 95
Macklin, Lance 43, 56
Maglioli, Umberto 70

Mairesse, Guy 43
Manzon, Robert 43
Maréchal, Pierre 34
Marshall, John 18, 40, 85
Marzotto, brothers 36, 70
Maserati 250F 69
Mercedes-Benz 69
Meyer, Olaf 97, 109
Meyrat, Pierre 43
Michaels, Paul 105, 109
Mimpriss, Peter 103, 104
Moss, Sir Stirling 18, 35, 56, 61, 62, 66-69, 70, 86, 94
Nash-Healey 34, 35, 38, 70, 95
Nicholson, Chuck 108
Nuvolari, Tazio 52
OSCA, 72
Palmer, Hugh 99, 102, 103
Panton, John 101
Parnell, Reg 43, 52, 56
Pearson, John 82
Rainbow, Frank 70, 72
Richards, Robin 39
Rol, Franco 34, 70
Rolt, Tony 34, 43, 52, 82, 85, 86
Rosier, Louis & Jean-Louis 43, 49
Rowan, Michael 100, 101
Rubirosa, Porfirio 43
Rutland, Brian 89
Sanesi, Consalvo 36
Schneeberger, Hans-Martin 82
Selsdon, Lord 40, 43
Serafini, Dorino 39, 43, 52, 70, 85
Simon, André 43
Simon, Yvonne 43
Skilleter, Paul 98
Smith, Bob 94
Sommer, Raymond 43, 52
Sunbeam Talbot 35
Sutton, Ron 13, 87
Stuck, Hans 34
Talbot-Lago 32, 43, 49
Thompson, Eric 43
Trintignant, Maurice 43
Van Damm, Shiela 35

Venables, Jarrah 107
Villoresi, Luigi 36, 70, 72
Walker, Peter 13, 18, 20, 40, 52, 68, 69, 80, 85, 86
Walker, Rob 69
Walters, Phil 43
Warburton, Guy 56
Watkins, Keith 56
Weaver, Phil 20, 22, 84
Weslake, Harry 12
Whitehead, Peter 18, 40, 52, 56, 69, 80, 85, 86
Whyte, Andrew 20, 39, 82
Wilkins, Gordon 92
Wilson, Donald 98
Wisdom, Tommy 13, 18, 20, 36, 52, 56, 66, 70, 80, 84,
    94-95
Wise, Tommy 94, 95